ON THE JOURNEY

Karen Kent OSU

On the Journey
A RESOURCE BOOK FOR CATECHISTS, CHAPLAINS AND ALL WHO PRAY WITH YOUNG PEOPLE

the columba press

First published in 2006 by
the columba press
55A Spruce Avenue, Stillorgan Industrial Park, Blackrock, Co Dublin

Cover by Bill Bolger
Origination by The Columba Press
Printed in Ireland by Colour Books Ltd, Dublin

ISBN 1 85607 530 3

Acknowledgement

I would like to say thank you to all the young people who have walked this journey of prayer with me over the last four years. To my Ursuline Sisters, our catechists and chaplains who invited me to pray with students in our Ursuline Secondary Schools. To the priests and people in the parishes where I have lived who invited me to pray with the young people of their communities. To Sr Marianne O'Connor, Congregational Leader of the Ursuline Sisters of Irish Union, who suggested compiling this collection as a resource for others. And most of all I dedicate this book to my parents who first taught me to pray.
Biblical quotations are taken fro the New Revised Stanrard Version, copyright © 1989 by the Division of Christian Education of the National Council of Churches of Christ in the United States of America. Used by permission. All rights reserved.

Contents

Preface

One of the greatest gifts of the liturgical reforms flowing from the Second Vatican Council has been the renewal of the Liturgical Year. Christian communities have been called to live ever more fully the journey of their salvation in Christ. Through the pedagogy of the Church's Year, Christians can see more clearly that the events of our salvation are lived in the everyday moments of human life. We are born, live, grow and die in time. The cycle of the seasons, the movement of the week and the rhythm of the day are truly places where we experience the love and mercy of our God. The human journey, the journey of a Christian community crisscross into the journey of the Liturgical Year. As the words of scripture are lived and contemplated in time, we become more familiar with the texture and shape of each season, we are brought more closely into the mystery of time itself and how it too belongs to God. The time of the heart intersects with the time of the community in the time of God.

The journey through the year is never the same no matter how many times we walk it, how many years we pass through its seasons; our lives are different, we get older, perhaps we may even grow in wisdom over the course of a year. The Liturgical Year is always new and there is a gift waiting there to be discovered by communities and individuals each time that we live its mystery. From the promise of Advent with its call to wait in hope to the crossroads of life and death at Easter time, to the celebration of the mysteries of the life Jesus in Ordinary Time we are constantly called to celebrate the mystery of faith in time. Contemporary culture has also added other significant times to our year, for example, graduations have become especially important for young people.

On the Journey: A Resource for Chaplains, Catechists and all who pray with young people by Karen Kent OSU, are the prayers and reflections of one woman who has walked this journey often, alone and in the company of

7

other pilgrims. She offers readers a sure map and a knowledgeable guide to the journey of the year. Not only does she provide a fine resource manual, she encourages other pilgrims to mine their own experience of walking this journey, to find the rich vein where their lives too have been touched by the mystery of God in time. Through her liturgies and reflections we catch rich glimpses of what these seasons mean in the lives of those who lived these mysteries – Mary, the Younger Son, the Woman caught in adultery, the people of Christmas. They are no longer just figures captured on a page or frozen in stained glass, they come alive in these prayers. They too are fellow pilgrims in the story of God's great love for humanity. The Word of God comes alive in these celebrations as it is prayed, sung and celebrated in the lives of those who hear it.

These resources serve both as liturgies that can be used in the worship of any Christian community, but also as models of how a community can put similar resources together for its own lived experiences and needs. While these resources were prepared for use with groups of young people, their appeal will be reach beyond this particular group to all pilgrims of whatever age who wish to celebrate the presence of God among them. In now offering these tried and tested resources to a wider public, Karen Kent has provided us all with much reflection for our celebration of the Year of Grace that is the Church's Year. For this service she deserves all our gratitude.

Liam Tracey OSM
Second Sunday of Advent
St Patrick's College, Maynooth, Co Kildare

Introduction

On the Journey is the response to many inquiries I received as I moved among the Ursuline Sisters in Ireland, meeting them in their ministries with young people, 'Have you any ideas for prayer ... meditation ... assembly ... etc ...?' Alongside this, as I spent a few years in our Thurles community the parish there also invited me to prepare prayer for and with young people and so this journey is also my own journey among young people.

This resource tries to offer a variety of ways to draw young people towards the sacred space that lies within each of us – the place where we meet God face to face in the everyday. It is an attempt to break open the words we are offered in the scriptures and make them come alive in the hearts and minds of young people. Many of them are tried and tested in schools, youth groups and parishes and I know from experience they work.

What the book aims to do is offer these to others who are in ministry as chaplain, catechist or those who want to draw young people into a place and time of prayer. Essential to any beginning in praying is the setting to which we invite others to come, therefore each of the 35 'prayers' begins by suggesting how the sacred space might be created using colour, shells, pictures, candles, cross, lighting and other ideas. Alongside this I always find a warm, comfortable place works well, with music playing as young people enter.

The journey of the book walks gently through the year offering suggestions for particular seasons of the year or significant times for young people. Some of the 'prayers' in the book simply require the leader to prepare a space and invite others to join them. Some though, require preparation in the form of preparing young people to participate as readers or taking the parts of the characters we meet in the scriptures. Some of the ideas are suitable for prayer in the parish church with large congregations of all ages and indeed came into being because a parish invited me to compose a 'prayer' for them.

I hope you will find my prayers helpful in your meetings with young people who I have always found to be open to hear the invitation into the quiet space where God is present with them and for them. I wish you a hope-filled, meaningful journey with young people through these 'prayers'. Feel free to adapt to your own situation as place and time differs for all of us but I pray you will be inspired through my journey to walk on with others.

Advent Prayer: Mary's Journey
Week one

Setting:
Mary's journey highlights Advent as 'Mary's season' and walks with her along the road to Bethlehem and the Nativity of Jesus.

It is intended as four weeks of prayer for classes – perhaps four assemblies or four class prayer sessions. It is perhaps best if the teacher is covering Advent with the class and the prayer is the culmination of the students' learning about Advent and its characters.

I suggest that a large centre piece be designed to include:
A blue cloth background; the road to Bethlehem made of stones; sign posts on the road marking the four stages of Mary's journey – the Annunciation; the Visitation; the Magnificat; the Nativity. Each week one student can light a candle at the sign post to mark the progression of the journey through the weeks of Advent. It might help to focus the students if a figure (perhaps the one that will be in the crib) or image of Mary is also included in the centre piece. At week four one might have the crib near by and one student can place the figure of the Christ Child in to the manger so completing the journey.

Leader:
Advent … the season of waiting … the season of Mary … the one who waited patiently … the one who sets the perfect example to all Christians … today we begin our walk along the road with Mary … today we meet her at the first junction on the road … the Annunciation …

Reader 1: The Angel Gabriel was sent by God to a young virgin named Mary, who was promised in marriage to a man named Joseph. Mary was at home, probably doing simple household chores when the Angel arrived …
> *'rejoice, you who enjoy God's favour!*
> *The Lord is with you'*

Leader:

Imagine this happening to you … an angel appearing in the room … wanting to speak to you …

Reader 2: What could this greeting mean … Mary was puzzled … angels didn't just appear like this … didn't she have to do something extraordinary or be someone special …?

> *'Mary, do not be afraid; you have won God's favour'*

Leader:

Mary sat … wondering … amazed … frightened … probably asking why me?

> *'You are to conceive in your womb and bear a son,*
> *and you must name him Jesus.'*

Leader:

Mary was stunned by the message of the angel … things like this just didn't happen … angels appearing … announcing the birth of a son … and not just any son … the Son of God …

Reader 3: The Angel Gabriel explained the birth would come about through the power of the Holy Spirit … Mary was silent … pondering these events … and these words …

Leader:

However afraid or confused she may have been … Mary as a faithful Jewish girl trusted … yes, her faith in God was being tested now but no matter how disturbed she was she heard herself responding …

> *'You see before you the servant of the Lord*
> *let it happen to me as you have said'*

Leader: Let us pray …

Today let us pray for all who face challenges in their life … that they will know the presence of God with them at this time … Lord hear us.

We pray for all whose faith is lukewarm that the message of Christmas will penetrate their hearts and minds this year … Lord hear us

We pray for all women who are expecting the birth of a baby this year ... may their children bring much love and many blessings into the lives of their families ... Lord hear us

We each come with our own prayers and intentions ... let us bring them before the Lord now in the silence of our hearts ... Lord hear us

We ask the intercession of Mary as we pray ... Hail Mary ...

Advent Prayer: Mary's Journey
Week Two

The Visitation

Leader: Last week we heard about the Angel Gabriel bringing his message to Mary from God that she was to become the mother of Jesus – the Son of God.

Reader 1: The Angel Gabriel also had another message for Mary that day …
'Your cousin Elizabeth, has in her old age
conceived a son.
She whom people called barren
is now in her sixth month.'
'For nothing is impossible to God.'

Leader: Elizabeth, Mary's cousin, a woman of advancing years was to become a mother. What joy this would bring to the family. For women to remain barren was believed to be caused by sins committed. Elizabeth for years had borne the taunts and insults that childlessness brings …

Reader 2: However impossible Mary had thought all these things were – she was in the hands of God for whom all things are possible. If God so chooses, it will become reality.

So Mary decided to go and visit Elizabeth … perhaps she would help her understand all these messages …

Reader 3: Mary set out the next day to the hills of Judea to visit Elizabeth. On hearing Mary arrive and call out her greeting Elizabeth experienced the child leap in her womb. Elizabeth, too, at this moment was filled with the Holy Spirit. She knew exactly what was happening and she spoke these words to Mary …
'Of all women you are the most blessed
and blessed is the fruit of your womb.'

Reader 4: It was at this moment that Elizabeth fully understood these events ... Mary the Mother of God had chosen to come to visit her ... Elizabeth was excited at seeing her cousin and sharing in her joy she proclaimed ...

'Blessed is she who believed that the promise
made her by the Lord would be fulfilled.'

Leader: These two women are central to the coming of the Messiah ... the one for whom the Jewish people had waited for so long ... the one promised by God to the people ... It is these two women who begin the story of Christmas ... as they faithfully undertake what God has asked of them ...

Let us pray ...

We pray today for all couples who are unable to conceive a child that they will find the strength to cope with the situation and never lose hope in God for whom all things are possible ... Lord hear us.

We pray today for all who travel to visit to bring comfort, hope and joy to others in times of need ... Lord hear us.

We pray for the gift of listening for ourselves and for all our families and friends that we, like Mary and Elizabeth, will be attentive to the voice of God in our lives ... Lord hear us.

As we approach Christmas we pray for all our own intentions today ... Lord hear us

Together we ask the intercession of Mary for all our hopes and wishes this Advent season ... Hail Mary ...

Advent Prayer: Mary's Journey

Week Three

Mary's Yes – The Magnificat

Leader: Last week we journeyed with Mary to visit her cousin Elizabeth and there we heard Elizabeth proclaim Mary as Mother of God …

Reader 1: Mary's response is to sing her song of praise …
My soul glorifies the Lord,
my spirit rejoices in God my Saviour.
He looks on his servant in her lowliness;
henceforth all ages will call me blessed.

The Almighty works marvels for me.
Holy is his name!
His mercy is from age to age,
on those who fear him.

He puts forth his arm in strength
and scatters the proud-hearted.
He casts the mighty from their thrones
and raises the lowly.

He fills the starving with good things,
sends the rich empty away.

He protects Israel, his servant,
remembering his mercy,
the mercy promised to our fathers,
to Abraham and his sons for ever.

Reader 2: Mary has accepted what is happening in her life … what is unfolding … but in accepting to become the Mother of God does she really know what the future holds for her son and for herself. Mary has stepped out in true faith … she has stepped into the unknown … trusting in God's providence …
And so she waits patiently for the birth of her baby …

Leader: Let us pray …

We pray for all families who are expecting the birth of a baby at this time. May these new born children bring much joy and many blessings to these families … Lord hear us …

We pray for the gift of faith for ourselves, that we like Mary will find the courage and trust to say Yes to God's plan for us in our life … Lord hear us …

Like Mary we too pray today for all those who are in need … the poor, the lonely, those in prison, those nations torn apart by war and violence, people of our world suffering because of hunger or disease. May they find comfort and strength in the message of hope that Christmas brings … Lord hear us…

Mary sang her song of praise and rejoiced at the news brought by the angel. May we too, like Mary, become willing messengers of the gospel in our world today … Lord hear us …

We ask Mary's intercession for all our needs today … Hail Mary …

Advent Prayer: Mary's Journey
Week Four

The Nativity

Leader: Today we walk with Mary on the last stage of her journey as she approaches the birth of her baby …

Reader 1: In those days a decree went out from Emperor Augustus that all the world should be registered. This was the first registration and was taken while Quirinius was governor of Syria. All people were to go to their own towns to be registered.

Reader 2: Joseph, being descended from the house and family of David, had to go from the town of Nazareth in Galilee to Judea, to the city of David called Bethlehem. He went to be registered with Mary to whom he was engaged and who was expecting her child.

Reader 3: While they were there the time came for Mary to deliver her child. She gave birth to her firstborn son and wrapped him in bands of cloth and laid him in a manger, because there was no place for them in the inn.

Reader 4: God's promise to the world is fulfilled through Mary … a young girl from Nazareth … who believed and trusted in the promises of God …

Leader: Christmas comes into the world … bringing light into a world of darkness …

The Son of God, the Bread of Life, is laid in the manger … the feeding trough of the animals. Bethlehem … the House of Bread … becomes the first home of Jesus, the Bread of Life …

Let us pray …

As Mary gave birth to the Son of God in her womb so we are invited to give birth to Jesus in our hearts this Christmas … making him known and loved throughout the world. Lord hear us …

Christ was born among the poor of his world … we pray today for all who are in need that they may experience our kindness and generosity this Christmas. Lord hear us …

At the birth of Jesus the angels proclaimed peace on earth. We pray for peace in our hearts, in our families, in our country and in our world and remember especially all people who live in fear of violence this Christmas. Lord hear us …

As Christmas approaches we each have our prayers and wishes for this special season … we bring these to Jesus today through the intercession of Mary …

Hail Mary …

Prepare the Way
An Advent Reflection

Centre piece: simple purple cloth and candles.
Background music, played throughout.

Introduction ... into period of meditation and quiet

Reading: Isaiah 40:3-5
A voice cries out: 'In the wilderness prepare the way of the Lord, make straight in the desert a highway for our God. Every valley shall be lifted up, every mountain and hill laid low; the uneven ground shall become level, and the rough places a plain. Then the glory of the Lord shall be revealed, and all people shall see it together, for the mouth of the Lord has spoken.'

Pause

We hear the prophetic voice of Isaiah calling out to us – an invitation – an invitation to prepare the Way. This is not a call to prepare for just any visit but a very special visitor – it is time to prepare for the coming of the Lord.

It is an invitation to look at ourselves ... to look within at who we are ... to look at our relationships with others ... to look closely at our way of life. Is there anything we need to change in order to prepare the way of the Lord. During Advent we are challenged to fill in valleys, to lay low every hill and mountain ... to let every cliff become a flat plain, every ridge a valley ...
But what does this mean for us?
What are we being challenged to do?
What changes are we being invited to make in ourselves, in our relationships, in our way of life?

Pause

We are invited to be made new again ... each Advent invites us to reassess

20

all aspects of ourselves and our lives. We are called into preparation ... preparation for Jesus Christ being born within each of us this Christmas. We are called to justice in a world where many people live in unjust societies, where many people are suffering because of the actions of others, where many people experience hatred and racism everyday, where many live in fear each day.

Often we are part of the building of these unjust societies and today we are called to look at how we as individuals contribute to the building of mountains and hills, to the formation of valleys and ridges in our world ...
Take time to reflect ...

Pause

Let us pray ...
That we will become the person active for change in our world ... become the prophetic voice calling out to others ... leading the way towards the straight pathway where we will meet Jesus Christ this Christmas in all his glory. Amen.

Advent Reconciliation Service
Prepare a Way for the Lord

Setting: soft lighting.
Centre-piece: purple cloths; sand; stones; tree branches; night lights.
Two readers, Presider and priests for the sacrament.

Presider: Welcome and introduction

Reader 1: Isaiah 40:3
A voice cries out: 'In the wilderness prepare the way of the Lord, make straight in the desert a highway for our God.'

Reader 2:
Desert … what is a desert?
What images does it conjure up for us?
A barren landscape; an empty place; a lonely place; a hot, lifeless space; a place where nothing grows; a place of no water; a place where no one can exist for long; an uncomfortable place …
Is it the place where you and I dwell …

Pause

When Isaiah challenges us to make a road through the desert … is he speaking to you and me … or to people of another place and time … people awaiting the birth of their Messiah?

Presider:
Today we are people who are busy preparing for Christmas … buying presents … sending cards … planning parties … preparing food …
Today we are people awaiting the birth of the Messiah … people preparing for Christmas …
Today we are challenged to make a road through our desert …
Where is your desert … what is in your desert …

Pause

The desert is the place in our lives where we are uneasy, uncomfortable ...
the place we keep hidden from others and from Jesus ...
It is the place that hinders our loving ...
It is the place that prevents us growing ...
It is the place that hurts ... because of our own actions ... or the actions
of another we cannot forgive ...
It is the hiding place of our talents and gifts ... those we fail to use for good ...
It is the place where we hold grudges against another ...
It is the place of broken friendships ...
It is the times we find it impossible to be grateful ...
It is the time we forget to say thank you ...
It is the time we are too busy to meet the needs of others ... the place of
our selfishness ...
It is when we fail to meet friends who need our time and a listening ear ...
It is the barren, empty, lifeless corner of our own lives ... the place where
we block Jesus from entering ...
Look hard into your own life today ... where is your desert?

Quiet music
(allow people time to reflect)

Pray together ... I Confess ...

For Advent to be a time of welcome ... a place where Jesus enters ... and
finds a welcome ... we need to come to him and ask his healing and forgiveness for the desert places of our own lives and invite him in ...
The Advent or coming of Jesus depends on our opening the door and welcoming him inside ...

Time for individual confessions
Priests available in various parts of the church
(quiet music)

Presider:
Gives communal penance.

23

Pray together ... Our Father...

Let us pray ...
Lord Jesus, we pray that our Advent this year will be a true time of preparation for your coming among us. We pray that you will find a welcome in places you have never before visited and that the joy of Christmas will abound in our community. Amen.

Reflection at the Manger

This simple reflection is intended for groups who are gathering gifts of food for the community (e.g. SVP collection) to come to offer their gifts in a spirit of prayer.
Setting: On purple cloth place the empty manger ... the animals from the crib ... place some candles around the crib. Students bring their parcels to leave at the manger.
Some background music ... you might sing carols ... offer prayers of intercession ... adapt to suit ...

Reflection
The gospels tell us 'come to me all you who hunger' ...
What does it mean to be hungry ... to have little or no food ... to not know where your next meal is coming from or when it will come ... or what it will consist of ... will there be enough to go round ...

We sit here today at the stable ... the animals around the manger ... their feeding trough ... where their need for food will be satisfied regularly ... they have no worries about food ... they are content ... they sit and wait ...

We too sit and wait through Advent ... preparing for the birth of Christ ...

What do our preparations entail ... buying presents ... writing cards ... decorating Christmas trees ... putting up holly wreaths ... wrapping gifts ... buying food ... preparing special menus ... choosing new clothes

Did anyone prepare the stable and the manger ... No!
Jesus was born into the ordinary everyday ... and was laid in the manger at Bethlehem because there was no room at the inn ...

Born in Bethlehem ... House of Bread ...
Laid in the manger ... the food container ...

Let us reflect on the significance of this ... Jesus comes into the darkness ... with most people unaware of the event in the stable ... But, think of the difference he made ...

He comes to invite us to join him in his mission … to make known the gospel message …

Today we bring here to the manger … our crib offerings … food for those who are in need …

Students place parcels around the manger

We like Jesus bring food and nourishment for others … just as he fed the hungry crowds who gathered … We are his hands and feet … the ones who give a share of our abundance and wealth to others this Christmas time …

The Christmas Gospel

Setting: This is intended to be used at the celebration of the Christmas Eucharist as the gospel. It offers an opportunity to involve the younger members of the congregation in the mime and the teenagers as the choir/musicians. The priest tells the story just as he would read the gospel pausing for the Christmas carols.
Characters: Mary, Joseph, Angels, Shepherds

A reading from the Holy Gospel according to Luke
In those days a decree went out from Emperor Augustus that all the world should be registered. This was the first registration and was taken while Quirinius was governor of Syria. All went to their own town to be registered. Joseph also went from the town of Nazareth in Galilee to Judea, to the city of David called Bethlehem, because he was descended from the house and family of David. He went to be registered with Mary, to whom he was engaged, and who was expecting a child.

Christmas carol: O Little Town of Bethlehem (verse 1)
During singing enter: Mary and Joseph

While they were there the time came for her to deliver her child. And she gave birth to her firstborn son and wrapped him in bands of cloth, and laid him in a manger, because there was no place for them in the inn.

Christmas carol: Away in a manger (verse 1)
During singing angel brings in baby hands him to Mary
who lays her baby in the manger

In that region there were shepherds living in the fields, keeping watch over their flock by night. Then an angel of the Lord stood before them, and the glory of the Lord shone around them, and they were terrified.

Shepherds stand to one side – looking terrified
A second angel stands before them

But the angel said to them, 'Do not be afraid; for see – I am bringing you news of great joy for all the people: to you is born this day in the city of David a Saviour, who is the Messiah, the Lord. This will be a sign for you: you will find a child wrapped in bands of cloth and lying in a manger.' And suddenly there was with the angel a multitude of the heavenly host, praising God and saying,

Christmas carol: Angels we have heard on high (verse 1 & chorus)
Angels stand to one side hands raised as if singing

When the angel had left them and gone to heaven, the shepherds said to one another, 'Let us go now to Bethlehem and see this thing which has taken place, which the Lord has made known to us.' So they went with haste and found Mary and Joseph, and the child lying in the manger.

Christmas carol: Silent Night verse 3 (all congregation sing)
Shepherds move to nativity scene to pay homage to Jesus

This is the Gospel of the Lord

Christmas Meditation

Setting: This meditation based on the Christmas story leads us to look anew at the Christmas story and ponder in a new light the message it brings.
Required: CD player, Christmas carols, background instrumental music, candles, slips of paper with the questions printed on them – enough for one per member of the group
Suggested centre piece: crib figures of Mary, Joseph, Jesus in the manger, Candlelight

Music: background instrumental

It is an age old story we've heard so many times before … yet if we really listen and open ourselves to its many messages may be this year it will hold something new for us …

The Angel Gabriel came to Mary living in Nazareth … a young girl betrothed to Joseph … The angel brought the message from God that Mary was to conceive and bear a Son whom she was to name Jesus - Son of God … Mary, even though afraid, said Yes to the angel's invitation … Joseph in his uncertainty agreed to stand by Mary and welcome the child … Mary in her fear went off to visit her cousin Elizabeth who too was with child … one who was to prepare the way for the coming of the Messiah … It was Elizabeth who first recognised Mary as Mother of God and responded with joy …

Mary and Joseph travelled by donkey to Bethlehem to register and while there the time came for her to give birth … the inn keeper welcomed them to his stable for there was no room at the inn … there in the humble stable the manger became the cradle for the Christ child …

The angels appeared to shepherds in the fields outside the town telling them of the great event … quickly they came to Bethlehem bringing a lamb as a gift for the family … there they worshipped Christ the new born king …

Some time later a star appeared in the east and the magi followed it to find the place where they too could worship the new born king ... they came to the stable bearing gifts of gold, frankincense and myrrh ...

As we ponder this story anew ... let the characters and symbols speak to you this Christmas ...

Christmas Carol: Suantraí
or other of your choice

As the carol plays we will pass around the basket. In it are the names of people and symbols that make up the Christmas story. I invite you to take a slip of paper from the basket and make this your meditation this Christmas ...

Christmas carol: Silent Night
or other of your choice

* * *

Questions:

MARY – she whom God chose to give birth to Jesus
　　　How do you give birth to Jesus in your life?

JOSEPH – who stood by Mary and helped her in nurturing the child Jesus
　　　How do you nurture those in your care?

JESUS – the One who came to fulfil God's promises to his people ... to live the Good News
　　　How do you live the Good News today?

MANGER – the feeding trough that became the cradle
　　　How do you adapt to the needs of our world today?

STABLE – the empty space that became the welcoming home of the Holy Family
> Are you willing to welcome all people into your space?

SHEPHERD – the one at the edge of the town who was invited by the angel
> Do you reach out to invite those who live on the margins?

LAMB – the gift brought by the shepherds
> What gift do you bring to our world today?

GOLD – the gift brought to represent the kingship of Jesus
> What is the gold of your life? How do you share your gold with others?

FRANKINCENSE – the gift brought to represent the priesthood of Jesus
> Do you invite others to come and worship
> through your living witness to Christ today?

MYRRH – the gift brought to represent the healing presence of Jesus
> How do you bring healing to our broken world?

ANGEL GABRIEL – the one who came on behalf of God to issue the invitation to Mary
> Do you invite others to come to know Jesus?

ANGEL – the one who announced the Good News to the shepherds
> To whom do you announce the Good News today?

DONKEY – who carried the pregnant Mary to Bethlehem
> Do you reach out to carry those who are in need in today's world?

ELIZABETH – she who recognised that Mary was carrying the Messiah
> Do you recognise the presence of Jesus in the people you meet?

STAR – the star that led the way to the place of Jesus' birth
    How do you become the guiding star for others?

INNKEEPER – the one who welcomed the strangers to his stable
    Do you welcome the stranger who comes to your door?

JOHN THE BAPTIST – the one who prepared the way of the Lord
    Do you prepare the way for others to come to know Jesus?

(You may need to have extra copies of questions if group numbers are large)

Meditation for Epiphany
Follow the Star

Setting: dark blue cloth; three large candles to represent the three gifts brought by the Magi; small white night lights as stars; background music.

Introduction and lead into meditation

Reading: Matthew 2:1-12

Pause

Reflection:
As we journeyed with the Magi ... following the star ... men who did not really know where this star came from or where it would lead them to ... men who trusted and followed ...

Many voices tell us to follow our star ... follow our dreams ...
But what is your star?
Is it the star of wealth and success ... of popularity... of prestige ... of fame ...?
Or is it the star of love ... of faith ... of caring for others ... of being a true friend ...?

Which star do you follow ...?

If your star leads to the manger ... to God ... it leads to love ... it leads you to care ... and like the Magi you too will be filled with joy.

Pause

Sometimes the stars in the sky are bright and clear ... on other nights they are dull and dim and maybe even hidden by the clouds ... or lost in the brightness of another star ... our life can be like this too ...
Sometimes we lose our way ... get lost in the clouds ... or hide away ...
Sometimes we are misdirected in our choices ... we follow the stars of Herod who leads us astray ... we lose our sense of direction ...

If we choose to be Christ-like we must follow God's star ... we must pay attention ... look carefully ... listen closely to the voice that calls us onward ... the voice of God is the Word of Jesus ... the forgiveness of the Spirit ... the Bread of Life ...

As you look to the stars ... look for the bright star of love ... of justice ... of truth ... the star that will bring joy to your life ... the star that will help you become like Christ ... the one that will help you to become a star lighting the way for others ...

Don't try too hard to understand your star ... accept it ... trust it ... know that it is yours ... that it is God's gift to you ... and only you ... it marks the path God has chosen for you ... it will lead you too to find the true King ... so follow your star ...

Reflection for Shrove Tuesday
Mardi Gras
Standing at the Crossroads

Setting: in the centre prepare a space into which you can build a picture of Shrove Tuesday ... you will add bowl of sugar; biscuits; chocolate; fizzy drinks; pancakes; charity box; map; background music to play throughout; appropriate song for the end.

Mardi Gras, or Shrove Tuesday as we know it, is a day of celebration – if you were in Rio it would be carnival time. If we had lived in the Middle Ages it would have been the day to eat up all the rich foods in the form of pancakes – a practice that continues today – will you eat pancakes today? Have you ever tossed pancakes from the pan? In England people celebrate today with pancake tossing races and much gambling is done on the winner and great prizes can be won!

(add the pancakes)

Or is today the day for giving up – the day for eating your last biscuit, enjoying your last bar of chocolate, glass of alcohol, spoon of sugar, smoking your last cigarette ... We continually use today as a day of giving up such things ... But *why?*
Is it to make us feel better? To lose weight?
Because it is something we always do?
And we give the money we save to charity ...

(add the symbols of the foods we give up and the charity box)

Let us go together to the crossroads where we can make the choice ...

(add the map to the picture)

Crossroads and turning points on any journey make us take a look at the map ... or read what an expert on the journey instructed ... or we look at signposts to check we are still on the right track ...

During every year of our life we experience crossroads days such as birth-days, anniversaries, meetings, milestone victories or losses in games ... these can all be turning points ... And so tomorrow, Ash Wednesday, is a day to pause a the crossroads ...

Let us stop for a moment and reflect ... we have before us examples of the 'giving up'

But what is the meaning of it all?

Ash Wednesday is a day of invitation ... an invitation from God to come and walk into the desert with Jesus ... to take time over the next few weeks to look at and ponder over the gospel map of life ... To come to a deeper knowledge of this Jesus person who walked into the desert to fast and to pray ... to prepare himself for what he was to undertake.

So too we can take this time to stand back, to take stock and discern what we can undertake ...

It is a time to get to know ourselves better and to come to the place where we can rest in God ... It also is a time to become more alive to the gift of life from God ... to become more alive to God and more alive to Jesus present in the world today.

So although the desert may not at first appeal with its dust, its barrenness, its lifelessness, it can also be a place to come and take off one's shoes and stand on holy ground ... to make a space where we can come to know and appreciate all that is holy in ourselves and to understand that we are chosen by God ...

So as we journey through these weeks of Lent ... let us remember to take time
   - time to reflect on who we are
   - time to reflect on who God is for us
   - time to reflect on Jesus in our lives
   - time to reflect on the love we receive and the love we give
   - time to become a pilgrim of love who is confident to enter the desert and be a guide for others so that desert time brings us to resurrection time

In this time of Lent, a time of penance, a time of choices made at the cross-roads let us offer all our mistakes to God – the God of love who turns them into opportunities and invitations.

Choose an appropriate song to sing or play

Ash Wednesday Liturgy
Distribution of Ashes

Required: blessed ashes; readers; music
Prayer focus: candles, stones, purple cloth, background music

Quiet music playing as people gather

Leader: Lord, you are merciful to all. Today, Ash Wednesday, we pray for the grace to keep Lent faithfully. May this season of repentance bring us the blessing of your forgiveness and the gift of your light in our lives.

Reading: Deuteronomy 30:15-16
See, I have set before you today life and prosperity, death and adversity. If you obey the commandments of the Lord your God that I am commanding you today, by loving the Lord your God, walking in his ways, and observing his commandments, decrees and ordinances, then you shall live and become numerous, and the Lord your God will bless you.
The Word of the Lord.
All: Thanks be to God.

Prayer before distribution of ashes
Leader: Let us pray.
Lord, bless us sinners who ask your forgiveness and receive these ashes as a sign of repentance. May we keep this Lenten season in preparation for the joy of Easter. Amen.

Distribution of ashes
(quiet music)
Turn away from sin and be faithful to the gospel

Prayers of the faithful
Lord today we ask you to turn to us with mercy for we have sinned against you.
Lord hear us.

In your loving care Lord guide the penance we begin today as we begin to examine the stony places of our lives and help us to persevere throughout this season in love and sincerity of heart.
Lord hear us.

Lord, guide the nations and their leaders according to your will – may they work for the common good and peace among all peoples.
Lord hear us.

We pray that the light of Easter joy we look towards may encourage us to be true disciples of your gospel message during this season of Lent.
Lord hear us.

Into your hands O Lord we commend all who died – may they see your face in glory.
Lord hear us.

Closing Prayer
Leader: God our Father, as we begin Lent strengthen us in our endeavours against sin. Walk with us on our journey towards Easter as we seek to live in union with you and with one another. We make this prayer through Christ our Lord. Amen.

Journey: Facing towards Jerusalem

Setting: centre piece might be made up of purple cloth, cross, stone/sand path way, candles. Use background music as required; song for the end of prayer time.
Required: two leaders; five readers

Lead those gathered into a posture and atmosphere of prayer

Leader 1: Jesus is now making his way through Galilee with his disciples

Reader 1: Mark 9:30-32

Leader 1: The disciples do not really understand what Jesus is saying to them. They are not able to really hear his words – and they are afraid to ask him to explain.

Leader 2: How often do we not understand just what is being asked of us? How often are we afraid to ask for clarity?

Pause

Leader 1: Continuing on the journey the disciples are really unsure what is going on with Jesus so they discuss amongst themselves and begin to argue.

Reader 2: Mark 9:33-37

Leader 1: Jesus questions the disciples about their discussion … they are unsure whether to tell him … but Jesus knew exactly what had been going on between them. So he continued his teaching to try to make the point to them that they are not actually hearing him at all. They are much too concerned about themselves – they are ignoring his teaching about the kingdom of God which they have been called to proclaim. The disciples are showing themselves to be quite foolish at this moment.

Leader 2: How often do we fail to listen … to really hear what is being said to us? How often do we think only of ourselves and forget about the larger picture of the kingdom of God?

Pause

Leader 1: A few days later Jesus is again setting out on a journey when a young man comes up to him with a question.

Reader 3: Mark 10:17b-22

Leader 1: The young man left Jesus and he was very sad. He just could not do the one thing Jesus asked of him. He had so much ... how could he give it all up?
Jesus tried to explain his encounter with the young man to his disciples ... telling them how it is necessary to let go of material possessions ... and to let God lead ... because with God all things are possible ...
The disciples ... particularly Peter are very distressed by this.

Reader 4: Mark 10:28-31

Leader 1: Jesus is trying to get the disciples to really listen ... to be attentive to all that is happening around them.
Jesus is inviting them to give themselves totally to the work of building the kingdom of God ... then they will be rewarded with much greater riches than they can possibly imagine ... the reward will be beyond earthly goods.

Leader 2: Do we really listen to God's invitation to us?
Do we say yes to the 'nice bits' – the words we want to hear ... and ignore the difficult request ... the bits we don't like ...?

Pause

Leader 1: Jesus reiterates his remarks about service ... about putting yourself last ...

Reader 5: Mark 10:43b-45

Leader 1: We are each invited to imitate Christ ... the one who gave everything he had. He let go of self to fulfil what God asked of him ... to be there for people ... to bring God's love into the world ... to begin the building of the kingdom of God on the earth...

Leader 2: It was not easy for the disciples ... they were unsure what Jesus was really about ... even though they had followed him and come to know him ... he still surprised them often ...

He challenged them to the very core of their being ... yet he loved them ... teaching them ... telling them stories ... yet at the end they still failed to understand ...

Leader 1: Lent is a time to re-think, to re-evaluate, to learn more about ourselves and our relationship with God and with other people. It is a time to get in touch with what we profess as Christians ... what we promised in baptism and confirmation ...

Leader 2: As we walk with Jesus through these days of Lent and into Holy Week ... as he makes his way to Jerusalem and ultimately to Calvary ... to his death ... we are invited to acknowledge how often we get it wrong ... how often we are more like the foolish disciples than true followers of Jesus ... how often we make mistakes, fail to listen ...

Leader 1: These times though are for us ... times to learn, to grow in understanding of our faith and the person of Jesus ... times for us to become more like God wants us to be ...

Let us stop ... reflect ... listen ... and take this opportunity to begin again.

Appropriate hymn/song: suggest: Could we start again please?
(from *Jesus Christ Superstar*)

Reconciliation Service
Cast the First Stone

Church might be in semi darkness ... light only on sanctuary ...
You will need readers as listed ... celebrant and priests for sacrament ... other
persons as necessary if the gospel is being dramatised (this can be a very effective
opening with practice)

Opening and introduction by celebrant

Reading and/or dramatisation of the story: John 8:2-11

Reader 1: Here we have a group of people, typical of many of us even today ... ever ready to judge the life and actions of another ... without stopping to look first at our own lives and actions ...

Reader 2: The Sacrament of Reconciliation offers each of us this very personal opportunity ... tonight/today we offer this communal celebration ... acknowledging that our personal actions and words always affect another and affect the wider community in many ways. Tonight/today we take the time individually to examine some aspects of our lives and open our hearts to God ...

Reader 3: we are here to examine our relationship with our family, friends and the community in which we live.

- Have I been unfair in my judgement of parents, children, brothers, sisters...?
- Is there a relationship that is damaged or broken that needs healing ... a relationship that needs someone to give way and say sorry ... to extend the hand of forgiveness ...?
- Is there someone who through my words has been wounded or hurt in some way ...?
- Are there family or friends I take for granted and expect to always be there for me and yet I fail to say thank you ... to offer something in return for their kindness to me ...?

43

- Do my actions affect my neighbours ... am I thoughtful, respectful, kind towards them ...?
- How do I react when I see the stranger in need ...? Do I pass by and hope someone else will come to their assistance ...?
- Do I care for the environment in which I live ...? Do I think about how my actions might affect the future of our planet ...?
- Am I quick to judge others before stopping to look inside at myself and my relationships and actions ... am I someone who, like the people in our gospel reading, is ready to cast the first stone ...?

Pause for reflection (quiet music)

Celebrant: Tonight is our opportunity to acknowledge and to confess our own failings to the God of love ... to open our hearts and ask his mercy and forgiveness.
I confess ...

Invite each member of the congregation to come forward to one of the priests present and to confess their sins and receive the sacrament of reconciliation. (During this time background music can be played)

Celebrant: gives penance to the community gathered

Sign of Peace ...

Our Father ...

Closing Prayer ...

Blessing ...

Reconciliation Service
The Prodigal Son

Setting: candlelight
Characters: Younger son; Elder son; father
Also: Reader and Narrator
Priests for sacrament of reconciliation
Required: large cross placed in sanctuary; three large rocks; stones for all participants; baskets for collection of stones (one for each priest); instrumental music during sacrament

As people enter the church or other space invite them to take a stone with them.

Narrator: Tonight as we gather around the cross we come holding stones that represent the rocks and stumbling blocks in our lives. As we pray together let us hold our stones and ask ourselves what do they hold for us. We gather together to express our sorrow ... together we ask for forgiveness ...

Chant: O Lord Hear My Prayers

Reader: Luke 15:11-14

There was a man who had two sons; and the younger of them said to his father, 'Father, give me the share of the property that falls to me.' And he divided his living between them. Not many days later the younger son gathered all he had and took his journey into a far country, and there he squandered his property in loose living. And ... he ... spent everything ...

Pause

Younger Son: Yes, I was greedy. I wanted to get out of home ... wanted my freedom ... my independence ...
I wanted a good time ... wanted to do what I wanted to do when I wanted to ... to be answerable to no one ... to have no responsibilities ...
I was selfish ... I was thoughtless ... I was careless ...

Pause

Narrator: Are you like the younger son? Does his story resonate with you? Are your desires the same as his?

Younger son lays his rock at the foot of the cross and turns away in shame

Chant: Jesus, Remember Me

Reader: Luke 15: 20b
But while he was still a long way off his father saw him …

Pause

Father: I have waited for this day … waited so long … waited for him to come home *but* since he went I have been distracted … neglected my family, my responsibilities. I have failed to notice all that has been happening here in the everyday as I stood watching and waiting … I was consumed by my one desire to the detriment of everything else …

Pause

Narrator: Are you consumed by one desire … by one project in life … ignoring everything and everyone else?
Do you forget to live in the present? Do you fail to see the gifts you receive each day? Do you fail to see and respond to people around you?

Father places his rock at the foot of the cross and turns away in shame

Chant: Jesus, Remember Me

Reader: Luke 15:28-30
He was angry and refused to go in … saying to his father 'These many years I have served you, and I have never disobeyed your command; yet you never gave me a kid to make merry with my friends.'

Pause

Elder son: I am angry … he got his share … wasted it … and we have a party to celebrate! What do I get? Nothing! Yes, I am angry, hurt, jealous … he always had it all … my younger brother …

Pause

Narrator: Are you jealous of someone? Are you eaten away inside with anger? Do you feel everyone else has a better life than you? Do you feel burdened by your responsibilities? Do you feel betrayed by those you love the most?

Elder son places his rock at the foot of the cross and turns away in shame

Chant: Jesus, Remember Me

Narrator: The story of this family is the story of every family. The stories of these people are our stories too. We are all human. We are all weak. We all fail in many ways.
But we know that we can come, place our rocks at the foot of the cross and ask forgiveness …

Please stand, holding your stone as we say together …
I confess …

Each of you is invited to approach one of the priests here in your own time to share with them your failings, then come, place your stone in the hands of the priest and receive the sacrament of reconciliation.

When all the participants have received the sacrament the priests take the stones and leave them at the foot of the cross.

One of the priests gives the communal penance to all

Narrator: Together we pray in thanksgiving for what we have received and pray for our own needs and those with whom we share this celebration …
Our Father …

As a sign of our reconciliation with God and with each other we offer each other the sign of peace…

Chant: Ubi Caritas

Holy Thursday
Reflection in the Garden

Background music – space in candlelight
Centre piece: cream cloth, bowl, jug, water, towel, bread, grapes, chalice
Required: narrator and 3 readers

As people arrive have space ready with music playing (you may prefer musicians or CDs)

Narrator:
Holy Thursday – we are gathered to remember … to recall the events of over 2000 years ago … the Passover meal had been eaten, Judas had declared his intentions and now Jesus leaves the Upper Room …

Reader 1: Mk 14:32-37
They went to a place called Gethsemane; and he said to his disciples, 'Sit here while I pray.' He took with him Peter, James and John, and as time passed he became increasingly distressed and agitated. And he said to them, 'I am deeply grieved, even to death; remain here, and keep awake.' And going a little farther, he threw himself on the ground and prayed that, if it were possible, the hour might pass from him. He said, 'Abba, Father, for you all things are possible; remove this cup from me; yet, not what I want, but what you want.'

Narrator:
We too have come apart this evening … to pray … to remember … to reflect …

Pause

Narrator:
Jesus invited his disciples to pray … they sat a little apart from him and watched and waited … wondering what it was all about … they had witnessed the events of the supper earlier this evening …

When any of us sits silently in the dark of the night we tend to let our

48

minds run over the events of the day … this day had been eventful for them … so as any humans in the same situation they were probably looking back over the day, particularly the evening. They had joined Jesus to share in the Passover meal – close friends together … as any close friends would do on this night … they had shared so much over the last three years … enjoyed the days walking with Jesus … learning from him … witnessing to his actions that brought change to the lives of many … and now what … As the disciples sat thinking back over the words of Jesus, let us too recall those words and actions here together …

Reader 2: Mk 14:22-24
While they were eating, he took a loaf of bread, and after blessing it he broke it, gave it to them, and said, 'Take; this is my body.' Then he took a cup, and after giving thanks he gave it to them, and all of them drank from it. He said to them, 'This is my blood of the covenant, which is poured out for many.'

Narrator:
We too sit and look at the bread and the cup of wine set before us…

Pause

During supper they had wondered what was happening when Jesus stood up

Reader 3: Jn. 13:4-5
Took off his outer robe, and tied a towel around himself. Then he poured water into a basin and began to wash the disciples' feet and to wipe them with the towel.

Narrator:
Here Jesus takes on the role of slave – washing the dust off the feet of his friends … not something the host would normally undertake … but he did it …
(This action might be performed here – depending on numbers)

Pause

Jesus is again setting example to his friends and to us all … to become servants of each other ... to be willing to stoop down to another ... to remove the dust from their feet ... and more than just washing ... but washing with love ... Jesus left the perfect example of love ... are we willing to do the same ... willing to become servant and what's more to allow another to serve us ... service for Jesus is loving to the end ... loving to death ... giving one's life for another ... if we call ourselves Christians we too are committing to this same love ... it is only in this way that others will know we too are disciples of Jesus ...

Pause

Tonight the disciples were still waiting, watching, wondering ... we know the end of the story ... but can we live the story today, tomorrow and in the days to come ... can Jesus say to each of us 'I call you friends' ... can he rely on us to 'go and tell the good news' ... can we come to Eucharist knowing that this is our daily encounter with Jesus our friend ... the one who gave his life for us ...

Hymn: The Servant King
A recording of this can be found on Feasts and Seasons – St Patrick's College,
Maynooth, released 2003. Music is included in the accompanying book.

This reflection was originally written for the young people of Holy Cross Abbey Parish, Co Tipperary in 2003

Stations of the Cross for the Young

Notes: This Stations of the Cross spans Good Friday and Easter Sunday. It is intended that the children and the teenagers of the parish prepare and pray it together with the congregation.

Setting: Church in darkness except for sanctuary area. Nine children and nine teenagers are required for the narration (marked Readers). Music group for the music and singing. Large taper candles for each of the children – one for each of the nine stations. Cross, for the veneration of the Cross at the end.
At the beginning of each station the child steps forward holding the lit candle – Reader (teenager) goes to ambo. All children and teenagers return for Easter Sunday.

The service begins with nine children in the sanctuary holding lit candles.

Leader: Tonight we gather to pray our Way of the Cross. Together we will walk the last footsteps of Jesus as he made his way to Calvary. The word 'station' means to stop or to stand still. A station is a place of waiting – waiting to move on, to travel to the next stop on the journey.
This journey we will make tonight – during which we will stop at the stations – is not only about the journey Jesus made many years ago it is also our journey of life. As we pray the Way of the Cross we reflect on life, our own personal lives, the lives of others and the events happening in our world today. The people who are part of the story are people just like ourselves, they too have their fears, their problems, their challenges and temptations in life, they too are sinners
And so together let us pray …

Chant: O Lord hear my prayer

The First Station: Jesus in Agony

Reader: Luke 22:39-44

Child: Jesus asks his Father to help him to be brave as he faces his pain and suffering.

Tonight we pray for all people who are suffering pain and agony. We ask you, Lord, to be with them as you were with Jesus on that night so that they too can say 'Lord, your will be done.'

Chant: O Lord hear my prayer

The Second Station: Jesus is Alone

Reader: Mark 14: 43-50

Child: When it came to the time Jesus really needed his friends … but they had left him alone. They had let him down. One had turned against him, another denied knowing him and the rest ran away.
Tonight we pray for those who are lonely, those who like Jesus have been let down by their friends just when they needed them most.

Chant: O Lord hear my prayer

The Third Station: The Crown of Thorns is placed on Jesus' head

Reader: John 19:1-3

Child: Jesus experienced spiky thorns being pushed into his head as well as the taunts and jeers of those making fun of him … which is worse?
Tonight we pray for all innocent people who suffer at the hands of others.

Chant: O Lord hear my prayer

The Fourth Station: Jesus takes up his cross

Reader: John 19:17

Child: The wooden cross is heavy yet Jesus carries his own cross.
Tonight we pray for all who carry heavy crosses … remember Jesus said, 'If anyone wants to be a follower of mine, let him take up his cross.' May we carry our crosses with courage.

Chant: O Lord hear my prayer

The Fifth Station: Simon of Cyrene helps Jesus to carry his cross

Reader: Mark 15:21

Child: Simon kindly helps Jesus to carry his heavy cross.
Tonight we give thanks for all who help others to carry their crosses each day. Is there someone we know who needs help carrying their cross?

Chant: O Lord hear my prayer

The Sixth Station: The Women of Jerusalem comfort Jesus

Reader: Luke 22:27-28

Child: The women felt sorry for Jesus when they saw him suffering as he walked the road to Calvary. One reached out and wiped his face … another cried for him. Jesus felt sorry for them.
Were they crying for themselves too? Often we feel sorry for ourselves … forgive us Lord.

Chant: O Lord hear my prayer

The Seventh Station: Jesus is Crucified

Reader: Mark 15:22-25

Child: Jesus, an innocent man, is crucified. His clothes have been taken from him. He hangs there alone … suffering … in pain …

Hymn: Were you there when they crucified my Lord

The Eighth Station: Jesus dies on the Cross

Reader: Luke 23:34-36

Child: Death is hard to understand … hard to accept. It is even harder when the one who dies is innocent. Yet, Jesus just asked his father to forgive those who were responsible for his death.

Chant: O Christe Domine Jesu

Leader: Tonight we come as one of those who loves Jesus, who tries to live life as a follower of Jesus. Tonight we come to show our respect to one who has died …

Tonight we come to venerate the cross on which Jesus died … died for us.

Veneration of the Cross
Cross is placed for veneration, children stand around it with candles
Background music during veneration

The Ninth Station: Jesus is placed in the tomb

Reader: Mark 15:46

Child: Jesus' body is taken down from the cross and buried in a borrowed tomb. The stone is rolled in front of it. The end … or is it?

Chant: O Christe Domine Jesu

All candles extinguished

Leader: Jesus is now buried … gone from the world. The question on the lips of those who were there is … what now? We gave all we had … gave up so much to follow him … what now?

Tonight we pray for all who have yet to know and understand the full story … let us spend time thinking of how we might become better witnesses to the events of Holy Week …

Leave the church in darkness with background music
to give time and space for personal prayer

Easter Sunday

At the gospel invite the children and young people back again to stand with candles unlit.

Read gospel of Easter Sunday – at the words 'he is risen' relight candles.

Gospel: Mark 16:1-6

After the gospel – link homily to the lighting of candles which will lead naturally into the renewal of Baptismal Promises. Invite children to pass the Easter light around the church.

Good Friday
Prayer around the Cross

Setting: darkness apart from candles around the church. Cross in the centre on the sanctuary. Spot light for the character when speaking, hanging head in shame for silence and when venerates the cross. Characters wear black and learn their lines. Narrator is unseen by congregation.
Characters: two women, four men, narrator

Opening Music: O Lord hear my prayer (Taize)

Pause

Narrator: This afternoon we commemorated an eventful Friday in Jerusalem that happened over 2000 years ago. A day that changed the course of history, but at the time did the people really realise just what they were witnessing … what they were part of … how it would affect generations to come?
Let us reflect on what happened … and how we sometimes perpetuate those awful events today …

Pause

Enter two women

1st woman: It was a great day in Jerusalem today. I've never been part of anything like it before and I've been at a few crucifixions in my time. Some say he had done much good in his short life but he didn't keep our laws and, what's more, calling himself the Son of God … who did he think he was?… we have been waiting for years for the Messiah and he thinks he can come the son of a carpenter and make the claim! Huh!
I'm glad I played my part … added my voice to the jeering crowd calling for his death … he had to go …

2nd woman: I don't know … he cured people, he performed miracles, he gave great example to all of us … and what did we do … we called for his

56

death … went along with the crowd … didn't stand up for what was right, for kindness, gentleness, for the one despised, for the one in need …

Two women turn to each other, hang their heads in shame

1st woman: Are you like me … afraid to stand up for the good … for the one who may be different from most people yet seeks to bring change to our world?

2nd woman: We can all hang our head in shame … we have all been too scared to stand out from the crowd … to set ourselves apart … afraid of what others would think of us.

Two women move to venerate the cross

Music: Jesus remember me (Taize)

Enter one man carrying the nails and hammer

Man: I was here this afternoon … with hammer and nails ready … as I do at every crucifixion … ready to make sure the offender was safely nailed to the cross … I don't usually think about it … it's just a job that I often do … take my hammer and put the nails through the hands and the feet …

Today I did the same … but a strange feeling came over me … as I hit the nails today and watched the blood come from his hands and his feet …
He was different from any other criminal we crucify … He has done much good, brought comfort to people … showed the way to those who were lost …

Turns and hangs head in shame

Do you ever think you made the wrong decision … that your actions have hurt and wounded another?… That's what happened to me today … I played my part in his death … at times we all contribute to the wounding of others … kick them when they are down … when they are at their most vulnerable …

Venerates the cross

Music: Jesus remember me (Taize)

Enter one man carrying board saying INRI

Man: I was there today ... played my part ... added a final touch to the cross ... put up the sign saying 'King of the Jews' written in Hebrew, Greek and Latin just to make sure everyone understood who this man claimed to be ... and I nailed it above his head for all to see.

I wonder why the Chief Priests asked Pilate to change what he had written ... He had made a claim ... said he was a king ... yet he didn't live like a king ... he lived a humble life ... worked with Joseph ... then wandered around the towns preaching, performing miracles, feeding the hungry, bringing hope to people in despair ... welcoming the stranger ... He was different in many ways ...

Man turns and hangs his head in shame

I labelled him ... even though I didn't really know him ... put up my sign for all to see ... gave him no chance to respond.
Do you ever label people because of where they live ... or the colour of their skin ... because of how they look ... or the way they speak ... or what job they do ... what they own or don't own ... we are all guilty ... we all label others without really knowing them.

Venerates the cross

Music: Jesus remember me (Taize)

Enter two men one carrying dice and clothing

1st Man: I won the game ... a spontaneous game of chance ... won the prize. I have his tunic ... we decided not to tear it so we gambled and I won. I'm glad I was there ... played my part in the actions of this afternoon ... I enjoyed the jeering, pushing him around, watching him struggle to carry his cross ... then being hung up to die ... naked on the cross.

2nd man: But why? What did he do? Did he really deserve to die? Was it right to take all he had, even his clothing ... to leave him with nothing ... I hear he was a good man ... did nothing to hurt anyone ... yes he challenged us ... but did he really have to die?

Turn together hang their heads in shame

1st man: Are you like me ... take pleasure is the sufferings of another ... take joy in winning at all costs ... no matter who gets trampled on?

2nd man: We are all guilty ... when a man is down we take all he has ... we enjoy the game ... we play our part in destroying another ... in leaving them to suffer alone.

Turn together and venerate cross

Music: Jesus remember me (Taize)

Narrator: Each of us can plead guilty today ... guilty of the same crimes committed on that first Good Friday ... we might ask what is good about it?

Pause

It was good because Jesus went through all the pain and suffering – carrying the cross while the crowd jeered and shouted at him ... when he felt the nails go through his hands and feet ... when he watched them cast lots for his tunic ... when they hung up the label above his head – he endured it all because he loved us ... loved us to his death ... a painful death on the cross ... and still we continue to commit the same crimes over and over again ... yet still he loves us and calls us to him.

Pause

We invite you now if you wish to come forward to venerate the cross ... to come as sorrowful sinners towards the one who died because he loved.

Music during veneration: Ubi Caritas et Amor (Taize)

It was a day of paradox ... in a moment of great evil the greatest good is revealed ... the forgiving love of the Father is made manifest at the moment of the ultimate human rejection as Jesus cries out, 'Father forgive them for they know not what they do.'

The same paradox exists in our own lives ... we destroy the love Christ offers to us in our words and actions to others ... today is a day to realise just how deep God's love is for us in the wounds of Jesus ... in his death for us ... the ultimate act of love ... to die for love of friends.

It is because of this love that together we can pray the prayer that Jesus taught the disciples ... the prayer he left for all people ... it is our prayer of thanksgiving ... our prayer of petition ... our prayer of contrition ... Our Father ...

Background music on CD

Please feel free to remain here in prayer for as long as you wish...

This Good Friday Prayer around the Cross was originally written for the Parish of the Cathedral of the Assumption, Thurles in 2003.

Prayer around the Cross
with those who stayed

Setting: Large wooden cross with spotlight on it. Area in candlelight only.
Required: 4 characters and 1 narrator. Mary, John and Veronica are sitting to
one side of the Cross – the centurion stands to the other side ... watching them
watching the cross. The narrator is unseen – sitting in congregation with micro-
phone. Characters learn their parts so that delivery is natural and conversation
like. All wear black outfits.

Narrator: Gathered around the cross on this Good Friday evening with
those who stayed ... with those who heard Jesus say to his Father, 'Father,
into your hands I commend my spirit' and they witnessed Jesus breathe his
last.

Silence

But why do we stay around ... watching ... waiting ... listening ... praying.

Chant: Stay here and keep watch with me

Veronica steps forward from the group and moves to centre

Veronica: I took my shawl to wipe his face as he carried his cross – to cool
his sweat-ridden brow ... Yes, Veronica's my name.
I stepped out from a group of women friends and bravely walked into the
menace. I closed my eyes and ears to what was happening around me – if
I hadn't I wouldn't have had the courage to go towards him to reach up and
wipe the blood from his face – was it just my shawl wiping away the blood
or was it a touch which said ...'I care'?
As soon as I looked at him I forgot all about the insults and jeers being
shouted at me by the crowd ... In that sacred moment I remembered his
words, 'Whatever you do to the least of my people that you do for me.'

Silence

Veronica turns to venerate the Cross ...
then turns to face the congregation

So why do you stay?
Are you like me, Veronica, willing to step out amid taunts and jeers to reach into another's pain ... to be the one who goes against peer pressure to step out in love for another ... to make a difference ... to lighten another's burden ... to ease their suffering ... to say 'I care'?

Chant: Ubi Carits et Amor

John moves forward to centre

John: I was his friend for many years ... we grew up together ... John's the name. As I stood here today the memories came flooding back ... the heart to heart conversations we shared ... the laughter ... the enjoyment ... the living ... the plans we made about how we would change the world ... me with my ideas and dreams and he with his actions. I wanted to shout at them – stop beating my friend ... stop mocking him ... jeering him ... wounding him ... and then I remembered he once said, 'No one has greater love than to lay down life for friends.'

Pause

So I stood beside him today just as we had stood together through childhood ... teenage years and into adulthood ...
I gave him friendship to the end ... and he gave me the courage to stay.

Silence

John turns to venerate the cross
then turns to face the congregation

But you ... why do you stay?
We all need friends ... but how much do we value them?
We all need companions who share with us the ups and downs of life ... who are always there for us ... no matter what ...
Friends who challenge us to grow ... to become ...and yet accept us just as we are ...

Pause

But how often do you say thank you for the gift of friendship ... for the gift of love?

Chant: Ubi Caritas et Amor

Centurion steps forward

Centurion: I am here tonight because I have to be ... it is my job ... me, I am the centurion. A job I will fulfil ... as always after every crucifixion.

I stand here ... slightly away from the small group that remain ... watching them ... watching me ... looking at the cross ... wondering why? What am I missing here?

Pause

I didn't really know him ... only heard about this Jesus of Nazareth. Yet today something stirred within me ... questions came to my mind ... what did he do to deserve this cruel death?
I was troubled by what I saw ... yet I was only here out of duty in the beginning ... but now at the end I want to stay here ... to be here ...
I recall my own words now as I stood watching this afternoon, 'Truly, this man is the Son of God.'
I really mean these words now ... but before I was just an innocent bystander doing my duty.

Silence

*Centurion venerates the cross
then turns to face the congregation*

But you, why are you here now?
Is it out of duty ... is it because you feel you ought to be here ... that it is the right thing to do ... or because others might comment on your absence?

Pause

Or are you here tonight because you are committed ... because you too believe that 'Truly, this man is the Son of God'?

Chant: O Christe Domine Jesu

Mary steps forward to centre

Mary: I am his mother – Mary's the name.
I once responded to a call ... said a prayer ... 'My soul glorifies the Lord and my spirit rejoices in God my Saviour' ... that day was a big risk to say yes to God not knowing where it would lead me. Yet, here I am today ... Today words just wouldn't come ... I could only stand and watch ... my heart was heavy, my spirit was sad ...

Pause

As he was taken down from the cross I held my son for one last time and then he was taken away from me. I took one last look at him and remembered his words, 'Neither death nor life can take him away from me.'

I am his mother ... the mother of Jesus ... the Son of God...

Silence

Mary turns to venerate the cross
then turns to face the congregation

But you, why do you stay?
Are you staying beside a friend in his dying moments ... comforting those who mourn the loss of a loved one?
We all experience sitting with those in pain ... sharing their suffering ... we stand with them as we stand here tonight ... out of love.

Chant: O Christe Domine Jesu

Narrator: Tonight gathered around the cross ... in prayer ... in love ...
We surround Veronica, John, the Centurion and Mary united in our sorrows ... in our pain ... in our anger ... in our hurt ...

We stand together in friendship ... in hope ... in love ...

Together we stand here united around the cross of Jesus ... we ask him to remember us ... to be with us in our remembering...

Together we come forward to venerate the cross … to touch it or kiss it … bringing with us whatever is echoing in our hearts tonight … we come forward to acknowledge our desire to stay … to be with Jesus … in whom love begins …

Chant: Jesus, Remember Me

Veneration of the Cross by all

Closing Prayer:
As we stand together we acknowledge our unity as one family and pray together the prayer Jesus taught us … our prayer of petition … our prayer of forgiveness … our prayer of thanksgiving …
Our Father …

Leave the church in candlelight with background music playing
Allow people to stay as long as they wish

This Good Friday prayer was originally written for the parish of the Cathedral of the Assumption, Thurles.

Through a Mother's Eyes

This meditation would be particularly suitable for use on Good Friday night in a candle lit time of prayer.
Centre piece: the empty cross – with spotlight on it.
Five characters are required – it would be good if they learnt the parts and spoke rather than read the text.
Mary sits to one side of the Cross and the other characters sit on the other side away from her. The Narrator is unseen, if possible is part of the congregation with a microphone.
Where music is required please choose either organ/keyboard or CD of reflective music.

Music

Mary: I sit here tonight alone … weeping for my Son … for all the times we shared as a family … for the joys of family life … the joys of rearing children … Yes I knew it was different for me … for him, but nothing could have prepared me for today.

Today I stood at a distance quietly watching the events unfold before me …

I sit here now in the darkness remembering the people … their words … their actions.

I recall hearing of last night … a night of remembering the joys of the Passover … he shared the meal with friends but then the unexpected happened … Judas …

Judas: I was offered money … 30 pieces of silver … I couldn't resist … it was too much to give up … so I did it … I handed him over … betrayed a friend for money …

Pause

Narrator: We are all tempted in many ways … tempted by the lure of riches and all that they can buy …

tempted by its attractiveness ... by all that it means in our consumer society ... We all seek to better ourselves ... but is it at the expense of another ... of a friend ... of someone who was part of our lives in so many ways ... when the choice is to be made, do we choose money and possessions over people ... over family ... over friends?

Music

Mary: I was around today when his friend denied him ... just as he had predicted he would ... Peter denied even knowing him, even after spending so much time with him ...

Peter: I let myself down today ... let down a friend ... a friend who has always meant so much to me ... a friend who gave me so much since that first day out fishing when the catch was so big it needed two boats to bring it ashore ... and yes I followed him ... looked up to him ... and now he is gone ... and I didn't even stand by him in his hour of need.

Pause

Narrator: How often do we deny knowing someone because of what others might think of us ... because of what might happen to us?
How often have we let down a friend?
How often have we turned our backs on someone in need?

Music

Mary: I could only stand and watch this afternoon as the crowd pushed and jostled and shouted for his crucifixion ... my Son ... they wanted him on the cross ...

Woman in crowd: It was easier to go along with the crowd than to be different. Everyone was there ... waiting to see who would be set free and who would be crucified. I got caught up in the excitement of it all ... the shouting, the cheering ...

Pause

Narrator: We all do it ... go with crowd because we are afraid to be different ... afraid to stand alone ... even though we know the crowd are in the wrong ... it is easier to go with the group ...

Music

Mary: Then Pilate, listening to the crowd, made his decision ... to free Barabbas and to crucify my Son ... it had taken a while for Pilate to decide but he went with the crowd ... and my Son went to the cross ...

Pilate: I didn't know what to do ... the crowd made their choice as is the custom at Passover time ... they called for Barabbas to be released and for Jesus to be crucified ... I was only trying to satisfy the crowd ... so it had to be ...

Pause

Narrator: It wasn't easy for Pilate ... it's often not easy for us ... we are faced with choices everyday ... but what informs our choice ... is it our need for acceptance and popularity?... our need to do what others want even though it may cause suffering to another?

Music

Mary: It is another story looking through my eyes ... I watched my Son ... innocent though he was ... accept death on a cross ...
A death because of others ... a death in which he called out and committed his spirit to his Father ... and it was all over.
I held my Son for one last time and then they took away his body and laid it in the tomb ...

Narrator: Today we are all guilty of the same sins ... we share in the guilt of Judas, of Peter, of the woman and of Pilate ...
We stand before God asking forgiveness for our sins ... for our guilt ...
We look on at Mary ... the Mother who stood by helpless watching the story unfold ...
We ask her intercession for us in our hour of need as we too stand at the foot of the cross remembering what happened today ...

Prayer: Hail Mary ...

Music

You are invited to remain here in prayer for as long as you wish ...

This Good Friday Prayer was prepared and first prayed by the Ursuline Community, Waterford. Good Friday 2005.

He is Risen ... Alleluia!
Prayer for Eastertide

Setting: plain wooden cross; white cloth; paschal candle; loaf of bread – broken in baskets for distribution; background music;
Required: Narrator; 3 readers; musicians for chants/hymns

Chant: Surrexit Christus, alleluia (sung)

Narrator: Christ is risen, alleluia!
But how do we know ... what really happened ... we read in the gospels of the many people who came to the tomb after his burial ... they found an empty tomb ...

No one saw Jesus rise from the dead ... but he appeared to them ... he had said, 'Tell them to go before me to Galilee ... I will see them there.' But the disciples hid away in the Upper Room ... afraid, unsure, wondering, what now ... they had given up so much to follow him ... now he was gone ... but Easter Sunday completes the story of faith ... let us join with those who were there and share their story ...

Mary Magdalene: I went to the tomb early on the Sunday morning ... I was so sad ... my Lord, my friend had been taken away ... crucified ... an innocent man ... Since Friday I have shed my tears ... I approached and saw the empty tomb ... the linen cloths lying on the ground ... the stone rolled away ... where have they taken him too?

Pause

I saw a man nearby ... presuming him to the gardener I pleaded with him to tell me where they taken his body to ... and then ... he spoke to me ... I couldn't believe it ... could it be him?... was it Jesus ... standing here, talking to me?
And then he invited me to go and tell the others ... Jesus is risen from the dead ...

Chant: Surrexit Christus, alleluia (sung)

Narrator: It was eyes of faith that allowed Mary Magdalene to see Jesus before her in the garden ... she saw ... she recognised ... she went to tell ... He is risen, alleluia ...

Surrexit Christus, alleluia (music only)

Disciples on the Road: We were walking home ... wondering how did it all go so wrong ... Jesus, crucified ... the one who promised so much ... gone ... buried in a borrowed tomb ... what was the point in hanging around ... the dream that held so much promise for us ... for so many people ... was over ...

Pause

And then a stranger appeared alongside us ... he seemed to know nothing of the events in Jerusalem of the last few days ... we told him all that had happened ... as we spoke he listened and then called us foolish ... and he went to leave us ... something told me to ask him to stay ... it was getting late ... he came to my house ... we shared a meal and then ... he took the bread ... blessed it ... broke it ... gave it to us ... just as he had on the night before he died ... we saw him ... we recognised him ... Jesus is risen ... he is here with us ... alleluia!

Chant: Surrexit Christus, alleluia (sung)

Narrator: With eyes of faith they saw Jesus sitting at table with them ... they recognised him in the breaking of bread ... they knew then as they had walked along the road to Emmaus with him their hearts were burning within ... they returned to Jerusalem ... to tell the others ... Jesus is risen, alleluia ...

Surrexit Christus, Alleluia (music only)

Peter: A group of us had decided life had to return to normal so once again we went fishing on the Sea of Tiberias ... we fished all night and at day break we returned to the shore with nothing ... a man stood there ... a stranger ... he called out to us to cast out the net to the right side of the boat ... we did ... we had nothing to lose ... then we had such a big catch we needed help to bring it in ... as I looked up again I realised it was Jesus, standing there on the beach ...

Pause

I raced towards him ... he invited us to breakfast and there he took bread ... blessed it ... broke it ... gave it to us ... as he had done the night before he died ... It was him ... Jesus is risen from the dead ... alleluia!

Chant: Surrexit Christus, alleluia (sung)

Narrator: Peter's eyes were opened ... he looked with eyes of faith ... led the disciples to recognise Jesus ... risen from the dead ... together they celebrated ... alleluia!

Surrexit Christus, alleluia (music only)

Tonight/Today we give thanks for the eyes of faith of Mary Magdalene ... of the two disciples on the road to Emmaus ... of Peter ... those who recognised Jesus and came to tell us ... he is risen from the dead ... alleluia ...

We are each invited now to come forward to reverence the empty cross and take bread from the baskets ... we too come with eyes of faith to say ... He is risen, alleluia!

Easter Music playing as congregation come forward

Conclusion:
Let us sing together our Easter Hymn:
>   *Christ is alive with joy we sing*
>   *Christ the Lord is risen today*
or other suitable hymn.

The search for new recruits
A text for use on Vocation Sunday
or by those involved in Vocations Ministry

Setting: The local employment office
Characters: Narrator (N); recruitment office staff (R); employer (E); possible recruits.
The recruitment office staff draw possible recruits from the congregation/group to present to the employer as the sketch moves along.

N: We are going back in time now to … (insert date) 32AD
What is happening in the world? Fishing and farming are probably the main sources of income for the people or working for the Romans … the women here in Galilee and the surrounding areas well … they are at home minding the children, keeping the house.
Most people follow some religion … there are Jews and Samaritans and others … all very faithful to their own particular way of life …
But change is in the air … something new is happening … new ways … new ideas … right here among us …
Let us go over to the local employment office to see what is really happening in the world of work here today…

R: Welcome! How can we be of assistance to you today?

E: I am looking to put together a team of people to assist with a building programme … we need to expand our original team of twelve …

R: So you want builders, carpenters, plasterers, architects and such like and perhaps a site foreman …

E: Well not exactly … rather a team who can work together to bring our company message to the people of our time … people who will continue the work of our founder and his original team of twelve who have worked closely with him for a while now …

R: hmmm … I see … I am sure we must have a few people who might be willing to join your new venture …
We have a young man, from a wealthy background, has enjoyed life to the full but now is back in the area, reformed and willing to do anything, even become a servant to his own father …

E: His name …

R: The prodigal son

E: Willingness to take on any task, very important, acceptance of past wrongs and willing to move on, to try again … okay I'll take him on.

R: What about this woman … older, mature, wise, known for her prophecies … shows extreme patience when waiting for projects to unfold … could be good … provide a balance to the young man before …

E: She would be?

R: Anna, the Prophetess … waited patiently … then prayed in thanksgiving for what she received … a woman of deep faith …

E: Great, she would be good to have around … prayer … very important.

R: And what about this man … looking for a new job … has been a tax collector … hated by many … known for taking more than his due but he has seen the error of his ways … is looking for another chance … will you be the one to offer him a new start?

E: His name?

R: Zacchaeus … please be the one to offer him a welcome, to offer the hand of reconciliation.

E: Okay … he can come and join us too.

R: And here's another woman … highly committed … extremely generous, gave all she had and that was only two small coins to the temple … a widow … no ties or commitments …

E: Commitment, essential to any group … generosity of heart … a must … I'll take her on

R: Two more women come to mind … often seen working together … a good team … wealthy … all the right connections … willingness to help …

E: Maybe we need those kind of people too … help spread our message among the wealthy of the towns … thank you … their names …

R: Susanna and Joanna. And what about this woman … not from the area … an outsider … rejected by many … seeking acceptance … would you give her a chance?

E: Could my group embrace her … find her a task too? I'm not too sure.

R: Just a small job … the messenger girl?

E: Okay I'll give her a trial period … see how she goes about proclaiming the message we have to bring to the world … it's new, it's challenging … let's see how she goes … Her name?

R: She is the Samaritan Woman, at the well …

E: Thank you, that will be enough for today … the prodigal son, Anna the Prophetess, Zacchaeus, widow with her mite, Susanna and Joanna, the Samaritan Woman.

R: Thank you too … I am so pleased to be able to assist your new project.

N: So you see back in those days Jesus invited a wide variety of people, men and women, old and young, to become messengers of the gospel … to bring the good news to others … used them as examples when telling his stories to help teach people his new way … the Christian way of life …

Jesus continues to call today … he calls each of us here to become bearers of the good news … some he calls in a special way …

Who is he calling? May be it is you? Listen for his invitation …

This text was originally prepared for a Vocations Day with the students of Ursuline Secondary School, Cork

Listen

To settle the group and enter into the atmosphere of prayer, play gentle music … this will continue in the background during the prayer.

'Let us listen for the voice of the Lord…
and enter into his peace…'
*(as the music is playing in the background
repeat this phrase intermittently a few times)*

Our world today is full of noise …
    the constant hum of the traffic on our roads
    the roar of aeroplanes criss-crossing the skies
    the ringing of telephones
    the many tones of the ever present mobile phones as text messages cross
    the globe
    the music of the computer games
    message alerts
    the radio or the television playing away in the background of life
    the chatter of people connecting with each other
    the music of personal stereos ringing in our ears …

We are constantly surrounded by noise … constantly waiting for the next sound to alert us to a friend calling, a text coming through, an email, a caller at the door. We are constantly waiting for the call to an important appointment, the invitation from a friend …

In the midst of all this noise do we ever take time to listen for voice of God?

Pause

Let us listen now … and enter into his peace …

What is God calling us into today?

Pause

Over the centuries God has constantly called people in a variety of ways for a variety of reasons …
Today we honour the memory of some of their responses …

We honour the call of Jeremiah … he who protested that he was too young to respond to God's invitation … and yet when he did God supplied him with eloquent words to bring to the people …

We honour the call of Isaiah who was afraid to say yes … and yet God took him by the hand, walking with him throughout the land …

We honour the wisdom of Elizabeth and Zechariah who in their old age, when they thought all hope was gone … listened and accepted God's will for them that Elizabeth would bear a son and his name would be John …

We honour Mary … she who said the greatest Yes of all to God … a yes that would shape the future of our world …

We honour the call of the apostles … Peter, James, Andrew … and all who left everything and trusted in their call to follow Jesus …

And we honour the call of every man and woman who since then has listened to the voice of the Lord … responded with a resounding Yes … and found peace in living a life of discipleship of Christ bringing joy, love and peace to our world …

Let us commit ourselves today to taking the time to listen to the call of God … to the invitation God is extending to us in our lives … will we have the courage to say Yes … to take the risk … to trust in the call of the Lord?… then we will experience true peace in the Lord.

This meditation was originally prepared for Vocations Sunday 2004

The Path of Life

This resource is particularly suitable for sixth years or graduates moving on to a new phase of life.
Make a path of stones as a centre-piece in the prayer space with sufficient stones for each participant to take one away with them.
Use suitable background music – set scene for prayerful reflection.

Psalm 16:11
  You will show me the path of life
  the fullness of joy in your presence
  at your right hand happiness forever.
Repeat 2 or 3 times before continuing

From the day of our birth the Lord has had a plan in mind for each of us – the question is can we trust deeply in this plan – can we allow it to unfold and let the Lord take the lead in our lives?

We all have plans for ourselves … we all have our hopes and dreams … our hearts are full of own desires for particular things, situations, ideals … And this is good … there is nothing wrong in these plans we make … but how often do we sit and listen to voice of God in the silence of our hearts?

Take time now to place before the Lord your personal desires as you prepare to leave this place moving on to the next stage of life's journey …

Pause

Listen … what is God saying to you today?
Sometimes we ask God to grant our requests but the answer we receive is not the one we want to hear … did God get it wrong?
I don't think so! If we trust God and believe in the plan he has for us, the answer is right for us at a particular moment in time …
Allow it to be … don't give up … move on to where God is calling you … accept what God is offering to you … wait and see what comes, as the alternative is often something greater than you would have considered possible for yourself…

To live with God is to live in the present ... it is to accept the gifts he offers to you ... it is in the acceptance of the plan that God comes to us, walks with us as companion and guide on the path of life.

Today as you prepare to move on ... as you face pastures new ... embrace new challenges ... accept the future that is mystery to you ... let us pray for each other that we will find true peace and happiness and unfailing joy on our personal highway ... the path on which God has walked before us to make the preparations for our journey ...

Pause

Before we leave, I invite each of you to take a stone from the pathway here ... each stone represents one of us present here today ... take one ... hold it ... treasure it ... let it become a constant reminder in the days and months ahead that you do not walk alone on the path to the future ...
Keep the stone ... hold it as a memory of today ... of moving on ... of each other and the journey you have shared so far ... as you go your separate ways know always that God is with you ... it is God who will show you the path of life and bring you to the fullness of joy in his presence.
Amen.

Pentecost Prayer

Setting: Red cloths; some night lights lighting; other candles unlit at beginning; cut out flames; water; Paschal candle in centre – lit; taper candles to be blessed and distributed; music
Required: 3 readers; Leader; two characters Peter and John

Music: Background music as people gather

Opening Chant: Jesus, remember me

Reader 1: John 20:19a
When it was evening on that day, the first day of the week, and the doors of the house where the disciples had met were locked for fear of the Jews…

Peter: afraid, unsure, wondering … what now … where did it all go wrong? What happened? It was unexpected … death by crucifixion … that was not part of the plan … not what I thought would happen …

John: my friend … the one who promised so much … gone … crucified … buried …
What now … we gave up all we had to follow him … and now … he's gone … and here we sit … afraid … uncertain of the future …

Pause
Reflective music

Reflection:
Darkness, locked doors …
uncertainty … none of us like it …
Hiding away … wondering … what now?

As you sit here in the darkness … imagine … the disciples sitting in the room … doors locked … fear in the air … what would the Jews say or do now that Jesus, the one who challenged all that they stood for has gone … crucified … buried … the end of the dream …

Pause

Chant: O Christe Domine Jesu

Reader 2: John 20:19b-21a

And Jesus came and stood among them and said, 'Peace be with you.'

Peter: Incredible … Jesus … He is here…here among us … with us again … everything will be back to normal again … no need to fear … to hide away … we can get on with life … go fishing again … meet the people again … open the doors … let's go …

John: Welcome, my friend … we were waiting for you … welcome … Peace be with you … come join us … we were afraid but now you are here … we are together again … friends …

Pause
Reflective music – light more candles

Reflection:
Yes, it's incredible …
Jesus, risen from the dead …. here again among his friends … here with us. Among his friends again …

But will life be the same as before?
Will it be as Peter expects it to be … nothing changed … or will Jesus ask more of them … will he put more challenges before them?

As Jesus said … so we say to each other … Peace be with you …

Sign of Peace is exchanged

Chant: Dona nobis pacem

Reader 3: John 20: 21b-23
Jesus continued, 'As the Father sent me, so I send you.' When he had said this to them he breathed on them and said to them, 'Receive the Holy Spirit.'

Reflective music

Reflection:
An invitation ... a challenge ... Jesus sends his disciples ... invites his friends to go out ... to go out into the world ...
He gave his Spirit to be their guide ... their courage ... their wisdom in life ...
The Spirit ... his parting gift to his friends ... a gift to be used ... a gift that would enable them to continue His mission ... to continue the work of the Father that Jesus had begun ...
This invitation is for us too ...
Pentecost is a reminder to us of the gift of the Holy Spirit ... the gift given to us ... received by us ... to be used by us ...

Light all candles
Appropriate hymn

Each participant is given a taper candle to light from the Paschal candle

Prayer (say together)
On this day of Pentecost, as we take the light with us, we ask the Lord to banish our darkness that we may be open to the grace of your presence among us today. Bless our words and actions with the seven fold gifts of the Holy Spirit that we may be your true disciples building the kingdom of God in our world.

Priest/Deacon blesses the water

Prayer
On the day of Pentecost the men and women gathered together and were filled with the Holy Spirit and they began their work of proclaiming the gospel ... May we too follow the example of the first disciples bringing peace, joy and love to bear in our world *(sprinkle with water).*

All: Glory be to the Father...

Closing Hymn of choice

November ... We Remember ...

Setting: At the entrance to the prayer space have a basket with a candle for each person who will attend (make sure it is one that can be held while lighting). In the centre of the space place a selection of coloured cloths and a book stand to hold the Book of Remembrance. The room is best lit by candle light and with background music playing.

Welcome – stand at the door and welcome each person by name and hand them a candle

Today we gather to remember ... to remember those we love who have died ... to remember those whose life stories connected with ours in so many ways ... to recall people who passed our way and left their foot print in our pathway of life ...

Pause

Many of the names of these people we have in the days of November recorded in our Book of Remembrance which we place now in to the centre of our gathering ... we each know the names we took time to write on its pages ... the people who made an impression on us during their life time ... the people who gave of themselves to us in many ways ... the people who showed us how to love by their words and actions ... the people who in so many ways meant so much to us ...

They are parents, grandparents, brothers, sisters, aunts, uncles, cousins, friends, neighbours ... they are people who taught us, students of our school ... they are young and they are old ... each one them is part of our remembering ... each one is etched on our memory for a special reason ... each one of them was a gift from God who was part of our life ... each in their own way ...

Today we each come forward and light our candle of remembrance for them ... as we do this we recall each one who was special to us ...

Students come forward individually to take a light from the Easter candle

As we hold our candles ... we watch their flame flicker gently in the darkness of this room and we recall names ... faces ... places ... times and seasons ... special days ... we hold these dear to us in our memory ... today is a day to remember ... a day to recall and most of all today is a day to pray and to say thank you for all they gave to us during their life time ... a day to say thank you for the gift they were to us ...

As we listen to the words of this piece of music we remember ... and we promise there will always be a place for them in our hearts ... a place for each of them in our memory ... we will not forget ...

Music: There is a place (Liam Lawton)

We remember with gratitude...
We remember with love...
We offer our thanks...
We offer our prayer...

For all those we have known and loved and we pray that each of them enjoys the friendship and love of God who has welcomed them home to their special place ...

We pray
Eternal rest grant to them, O Lord, and may perpetual light shine upon them. May they rest in peace. Amen.

Students come forward and place the lighted candles into the centre piece (during this time you might re play 'There is a place')

Reading: John 11:25-26
Jesus said, 'I am the resurrection and the life. Those who believe in me, even though they die, will live, and everyone who lives and believes in me will never die.'

Blessing:

May the Lord bless each of us in our remembering, be our comfort in times of sorrow and bring us to joy in the knowledge that all who believe will rise with him on the last day. Amen.

Gratitude
The Parable of the Ten Lepers

Setting: coloured cloths; one large candle to represent Jesus; ten nightlights to represent the ten lepers; background music

Introduction to meditation

Read: Luke 17:11-17

Pause

Jesus meets ten lepers ... ten men who have been cast out of society ... had no contact with their family ... been unable to work ... had to beg for food.

Jesus offers them a new start ... he heals them of this dreadful disease ... he gives them a chance to return to their families ... to live again amongst the people they know ... a chance to work again ... to earn a living ... a chance of new life ...

But ... only one said thank you ... only one was grateful for the actions of Jesus ...

What of the others ... what happened to them?

Perhaps one was so delighted he went to meet his friends and spent long days and nights celebrating ... partying ... eating and drinking with his friends ... so delighted to be back amongst them again ... that he forgot to say thank you ...

Another perhaps was so happy to be able to return home to his family ... so happy to see his wife and children again and hear all their news ... hear about all the everyday family events that he had missed out on that he just didn't think to go and say thank you ...

May be one of them had been so angry that he had been excluded for so long that all he wanted to do was get back to a normal way of life ... it didn't even cross his mind to go to Jesus and say thank you ...

One of them might have felt that healing was what he deserved ... he had done nothing to deserve all that he had endured ... the exclusion ... the shame ... he had endured enough ... why should he say thank you ...

Perhaps another was just unable to understand ... found it difficult to return to his family and friends ... and he just wandered around in a daze ... unsure what to do ... he was so confused in his thoughts ... saying thank you just never occurred to him ...

Another perhaps went around boasting of his cure ... telling everyone ... but never accepting that it was Jesus who was the one who offered the healing hand ... he had no need to thank Jesus ... what was it to do with him?

Another ... well ... he was always saying he would go to Jesus tomorrow to say thank you ...

When we think about these men ... these men who for a variety of reasons did not say thank you to Jesus ... neglected to show how grateful they were for the healing action of Jesus in their life ... do we see any similarities?

They are probably just like ourselves in many ways ... How many times do you forget ... do not bother ... go off partying ... celebrating good fortune ... get so caught up in the everyday business of life ... promise to do it tomorrow ... that you like them forget or neglect to say thank you ... omit to show your gratitude for the good things that happen in life ...

And yet ... thank you can mean so much ... How many people who have been instrumental in the good things that happen to us have turned to themselves and asked the question ... what happened? ... just like Jesus when he recalled healing ten lepers and yet only one ... the Samaritan ... returned to say thank you and show how grateful he was to Jesus for being the instrument who brought healing to his life ... who enabled him to return to society ... to his family ... his friends and live again ...

Take time now to reflect ... who is the person you need to say thank you to ... perhaps there is more than one ... parents ... friends ... relatives ... teachers ... someone who helped you in some way ... to Jesus ... Thank you can mean so much ... In the depth of your heart now acknowledge who needs your thank you today ...

You Are Mine
Praying with shells

Setting: darkened room – candlelight – centre piece to include a selection of shells (enough for one each); background music

Welcome

… settle … relax … breathe gently …

Imagine you are at the seashore …

Peace can often be found while walking barefoot in the sand listening to the sounds of the sea … the waves rolling in and out … tides turning … the sun dancing across the water … the scent of the salty air filling your nostrils … the breeze blowing gently on your skin … blowing your hair …

As you walk you notice the variety of shells in the sand … choose one from the centre piece here … pick it up … hold it gently in your hands …

Look at your shell … its size … its colour … its shape … its texture …
Each shell is unique …
Why did you choose this particular shell from the variety available?

Each shell is different … it is unique …
God has planned it this way … plans the differences … plans the uniqueness of each one …

What was it that drew you to the one you chose?
It is different from the reason the person sitting next to you chose their shell?

Just as each shell is unique … is different from the next … each one is a shell …
In the same way each one of us sitting here is different … is unique … yet each of us belongs to the family of humanity …
Just as each shell is created by God … so are we …

We are formed by God ... created by God ... made in his image and likeness ... yet each has a uniqueness of their own ...

Listen to the words of Isaiah:

> Coasts and islands, listen to me,
> pay attention, distant peoples.
> Yahweh called me when I was in the womb,
> before my birth he had pronounced my name.

Just as God made you, so he called you by name...
What name did he call you? *(around the circle each one says their name aloud)*

God gave you as gift all that you are ... your talents ... your joys ... your sorrows ...
God is in each of you ... is with you ... just as you are ...
God loves you ... just as you are ...
God knows you ... just as you are ...

Listen to the words of the following song:

> *Choose either* You are Mine (David Haas)
> *or* Be not afraid
> *or* Do not be afraid
> *or any other hymn/song on a similar theme*

What are these words saying to you?
Time and space for sharing, either in the large group or in smaller groups

As we come to the closing of our prayer what is it that you would like to say to God in response to what you have heard today?
    Maybe you have a question for him...
    Maybe you are angry with God and need to share it with him
    Maybe you need to say thank you to God for his gifts to you
    Maybe you have a request to make of God...

Use this time of prayer to talk with God (this may be aloud or in private depending on the group)

Closing prayer

Let us pray today that each of us will always be aware of our own uniqueness created by God. We give thanks for all that we are for each other, for
our families, for our friends, for our world. May we use our unique gifts
wisely in the service of others and of all of creation. Amen.

Meditation
Walking like Moses

Setting: Cut outs of footprints (enough for one each); cloth; candles; background music; pencils; appropriate hymns on CD.
This meditation is probably most useful with sixth year students.

Introduction ... lead into meditative prayerful atmosphere

Scripture reading: Exodus 3:10-11

Pause – Read again – Pause

Moses was reluctant to take up the task God asked of him ...
He questioned God ... why me?
What if they don't accept me?

How often do we question the motives of the one who asks the question of us ... the one who invites us ... who challenges us?
How often do we fail to recognise the hand of God in the invitation?

We know that Moses did eventually take up the task and lead the people out of Egypt ... but the task didn't come without its trials ... its challenges ... many stones fell into Moses' path ... yet God stood by him just as he had promised and the people were led to safety ...

Scripture reading: Exodus 14:19-22

Pause

This success led them to sing their song of victory ... they had overpowered the mighty Egyptian army with the help of God.

Do we acknowledge the help of God in our lives?
Are we ready to commit ourselves to walking with God each day ... truly living the words we often say ... 'Thy will be done' ...

Today we come together to commit ourselves to walking with God and with each other during the coming year ... a year which will bring its own challenges and trials ... a year when we will need to know that God walks with us always … To acknowledge this commitment you are invited to each take a footprint and to write your name on it and, as we listen to the words of the song 'On the Journey', we place our footprints into the centre of the group …

Song: On the Journey (Liam Lawton)
or other as appropriate

Meditation
Listening like Jeremiah

Setting: cloth; background music; hymns on CD; pictures/postcards of doors/doorways/gateways; candles.

Introduction ... prepare group for meditative prayer time

Today we are going to take time to journey with one of the Prophets ... Jeremiah ...
Prophets in the Old Testament were those called by God to some special mission ... what they have in common is they found it difficult to say 'Yes' to God – they often fought with God ... hoping he would choose some-one else for the job ... Listen to Jeremiah's story ...

Scripture reading: Jeremiah 1:4-10

Pause

Spend some time with these words ...
What are they saying to you?
Do you hear someone calling to you:
Everyday we are called by another ... to help ... to listen ... to be with ... to be a friend ... to care ... to love ... in so many ways we respond to the call of another ...

Do we realise that behind all these calls on us lies the voice of God ... God reaching out to us ... inviting us ... challenging us ... confronting us ... asking us to take one more step on our journey ... calling us to new places ... new people ... new experiences ... wanting us to walk with him ...

> *Hymn: Be not afraid or Do not be afraid*
> *or other as appropriate*

God knows all and sees all ... he is in all that we are ... in all that we do ... in all that we say ... Do we recognise God's daily call to us?

Think back over today ... how many times did someone call to you ... how did you respond? With joy ... with love ... with anger ... with irritation ... with resentment ... with peace ...

In this your last year at school ... you are at a time of making choices ... it is like standing at the crossroads ... which path will you take? The path you choose will have a bearing on the rest of your life ...
How do you feel ... hopeful ... frightened ... sad ... relieved ... happy ... as you look to the future how do you feel?

It is like a series of doors before you, each opening on to something different ... all unknown ... all you have to do is choose the right one for you ... the one that God is calling you towards ...

Here in our centre piece are a series of pictures of doors and gateways ... take time to look at them ... stand up, walk around and look at them all ... then slowly, when you are ready, make your choice ...

Why did you choose that door ... what drew you towards it ... what is the question it brings up for you?

Give some time for sharing in small groups

Closing Prayer
O God, you who called Jeremiah and who continually call out to us each day be with us during this time of choices and decisions. Just as you have led us to the picture we now hold, lead us towards the door you hold open for us in our lives. Be with us as we journey towards our future ... a future that is mystery. Amen.

Meditation
Friendship

Setting: background music; candles; pictures of people; cloth; songs as appropriate.

Introduction ... prepare group for meditation

Today we are going to explore the idea of friendship ... something we all experience ... something we all need ... yet what is it? Why do we choose the friends we make?

Song: I'll be there for you (theme from Friends)

In the centrepiece are a selection of pictures of people ... stand up and walk around and take a good look at them ... then make your choice ... who would you choose as a friend?
Is it someone famous ... someone who looks like someone you know?
What drew you towards them ... their eyes ... their smile ... their face ... their clothes ... their figure ... their age group ... male or female?

Scripture reading: Ecclesiasticus 6:5-17

Pause

Now think about your own friends ... how long have you known them ... what drew you together ... what holds the friendship ... what makes it last? Do the words of Ecclesiasticus hold true for you today?

And what happens when things go wrong ... why do friendships go wrong ... are they repairable ... what are your own experiences of friendships – the good things about them and how sometimes they don't live up to our expectations?

Offer time for sharing experiences in small groups

Ultimately it is Jesus who displays the absolute friendship to us when he lays down his life for us on the cross ... he invites us to do the same ... take time to reflect on this challenge ...

Song: choose an appropriate song to close

The Artist's Palette
Meditation for the beginning of the school year

Setting: Either coloured cloths of red, blue and yellow or helium balloons of these colours (or a mix of both) to create a centre piece as focus for prayer. Background music; I suggest learning hymn/song about colours. Leader and readers for prayers.

Leader: Welcome …

Reader 1: RED … the colour of the rose given to a loved one; RED … the colour of passion; RED … the colour of flames in the fire; RED … the colour of warmth and welcome; RED …

Reader 2: BLUE … the colour of the summer sky; BLUE … the colour of the sea water; BLUE … the colour of peace and tranquillity; BLUE … the colour of comfort and healing; BLUE …

Reader 3: YELLOW … the colour of sunshine; YELLOW … the colour of spring flowers; YELLOW … the colour of encouragement and hope; YELLOW …

Leader: When the artist takes out his clean palette these are the three primary colours which he squeezes from his tubes of paint on to his palette. These three colours are the beginning of every masterpiece he creates. These three colours form the basis of all his work … the beginning of all the colours he will create by mixing them together to create new colours … he mixes the red and the yellow to create orange … he mixes blue and yellow to create green … he mixes red and blue to create purple … and so he goes on mixing to create new colours …

The beginning of our school year is much the same … the palette is the school and we are each a colour on the palette … as we meet together our colours mix together to create new shades in the painting that is our school community in this academic year … sometimes our colours will mix to create new shades of beauty that will enhance the picture; at other times the colours will clash … these shades are all part of the picture … the masterpiece that we will create together this year …

As we begin this year we invite God into the middle of our palette and ask him to be with us each day as we mix the colours to create new shades together …

Let us pray:

When we see the colour red we think of love, of warmth, of welcome. We pray this year that all of us will feel welcome here and that each of us will work together to make our school a happy community where all feel loved and valued for who we are and the gifts we bring to our school community.
Lord hear us …

When we see the colour blue we think of peace, comfort and tranquillity. We pray at this time for peace … peace in our hearts … peace in our families … peace in our country and peace in our world. We ask God to be with us as we seek to create a place of peace here in our school community.
Lord hear us …

When we see the colour yellow we think of summer sunshine, of hope and encouragement. We pray today that we will be happy together this year and be people of hope, always encouraging each other to attain our goals and to succeed in all aspects of life here in our school.
Lord hear us…

Leader: We give thanks today for the gift of each other and ask God the artist to be with us as we seek to create our masterpiece of love … of hope … of peace during this school year. Amen.

Closing hymn: Colour the world with a rainbow of love
or Colours of day
or other suitable hymn/song

School Assembly
'You are God's work of art'

Setting: multi-coloured cloths either in centre or hanging as a backdrop; paint brushes; blank canvas; some canvas with splashes of colour added; jars of water; paints; crayons.
Play background music as students gather.
Have ready either pictures for each student or painting for each class group to receive and take away as a reminder.

Welcome from Principal or other appropriate person

Reading: Genesis, chapter 1
Then God said, 'Let us make humankind in our image, according to our likeness ... So God created humankind in his image, in the image of God he created them; male and female he created them. God blessed them. God saw everything that he had made, and indeed, it was very good.' (1:26a, 27-28a, 31a)

Leader: Each of us is like a canvas ... waiting for the artist to add the next colour ... to paint the next scene ... Every moment of every day adds another dimension to the picture that you are. We each come here as unique works of art ... made by the hand of God.

In first year we come with a few colours on our canvas and every year we are here more strokes of the brush are added to our picture.

We are each the brush stroke on the painting of another ... as our lives touch each other each day we add colour and shape to another's canvas

As God's works of art we are created in the image of the Creator – of God – called to be like him – to paint a picture of ourselves that mirrors his own image – Jesus Christ.

As we begin this new school year let us be mindful as the days and weeks pass by that 'I am God's work of art' and to remember to say to another 'You are God's work of art.'

A work of art is to be respected, to be treated with kindness, with love, with generosity ... to be cared for – it is precious.

Like the paintings hanging in the National Gallery we too make up a gallery – the (*name of school*) School gallery ... each of us is a masterpiece from the hand of God adding beauty to our surroundings.

To remind us of this as we go through the year we will ...

either give each student a picture of a work of art or give each class a painting to hang in their classroom. (choose one to highlight the theme of the year)

This assembly was originally prepared for the students of the Ursuline Boarding School, Thurles, Co Tipperary.

End of Year Assembly
The Colours Added to the Canvas

Setting: backdrop of coloured cloths; canvas with splashes of colour; paint brushes; water pots; paints

As students gather you might play background music

Leader:
We began our year with the theme 'You are God's work of art' and reflected on the canvas that we are and upon which God paints the picture.

Let us think back to that day in September and remember the events of the year which we have experienced and shared together – each one adding another brushstroke to our picture –
Here mention the highlights of school year,
e.g. The first day in a new class – new subjects, new teachers
Music, sport, show, achievements, feast days, fundraising etc
And now we come to the end of the year – to exams, and look forward to summer holidays

What are the colours these events have added to our canvas?

Perhaps God has added yellow … the colour of encouragement which brings the reassurance that we all need within and around us to face up to whatever comes into our path … knowing as the psalmist says that:
> God is our refuge and strength
> an ever present help in trouble – therefore we will not fear.

Pause

Maybe God has added a blue stroke to your canvas – blue for healing – on those days when you longed for comfort and courage to cope with grief, pain or uncertainty …
In the words of the motto of the Special Olympics:
> 'Let me win, but if I cannot win, let me be brave in the attempt.'

Pause

During the year we have each experienced growth and embraced change – at these times God paints with green – green for growth and change – when decisions and changes must be made to accept the past and find the future …
In the words of John Henry Newman
    'If you are intended for great ends … you are called to great hazards.'

So let us embrace change, face uncertainty and take risks into the future that is mystery.

Pause

Throughout the year we have made new friendships and built on existing ones … in this God adds red to our canvas … red for relationships and friendships …
In the words of the Book of Proverbs:
    Some friends play at friendship
    but a true friend stays closer than one's nearest kin. (Proverbs 18:24)

Pause

So together we give thanks for the yellows, blues, greens and reds that God has added to our canvas during this academic year.

We give thanks for the picture that is emerging – the picture that is unique to each one of us …
And we move on ready to embrace the new colours that God will continue to add until our picture is complete …
We go safe in the knowledge that we are truly 'God's works of art'. Amen.

School Assembly
'Shine like stars in the world'

Setting: Background music; candles; blue cloth and cut out silver stars and candles for backdrop/centre piece; paschal candle

Introduction: (you might play background music as students gather)
Welcome given by School Principal (or other as appropriate)

Reading: Philippians 2:13-15
It is God who is at work in you enabling you both to will and to work for his good pleasure. Do all things without murmuring or arguing so that you may be blameless and innocent, children of God ... and shine like stars in the world.

Pause

Reflection: (read by Leader)
Shine like stars ...
... but what is a star?

A star is a small light that lights up the night sky ...
A star is a guide to travellers and seafarers in the darkness ...
A star helps astronomers and scientists predict the movement of the planets in the universe ...

Sometimes the night sky is full of bright stars ... other times the stars are hidden by thick clouds ...

Our reading invites us to 'shine like stars', to become like the star in the night sky ... a beacon of light for all to see ... lighting up the darkness ... lighting the way forward for others by our words and actions ... called to become the light of Christ shining in the world ... pointing the way towards God.

As we begin another school year ... some of you are returning to a familiar place with familiar people around you ... others are joining us for the first time ... a new place ... new faces ... new routines ...

Let us take as our theme for the year, 'Shine like stars in the world.'

So how can we do this together?
... by our kindness to each other
... by our helpfulness to another in need ... particularly to a new student
... by giving a smile or a kind word to one who is lonely
... by thinking of others before ourselves
... by setting a good example ... in study time ... in corridors ... on the games field ... in the classroom ... even if that means going against the crowd
... by accepting others as they are
... by acknowledging our own faults and failings
... by encouraging and celebrating the gifts and talents of others

Today we will light candles from this year's paschal candle for each class in the school

Light candles
Give one to each class ... either rep from class or tutor

Closing Prayer (when all have received candles)
We take this light from here today to remind us to 'shine like stars' throughout this academic year.

May the light and warmth of these flames be a reminder to us that we are called to shine like stars in the world for all to see. Amen.

End of Year Assembly
'When did your star light up the sky this year?'

Setting: blue cloth; stars on it; candles
You might play suitable background music as students gather

Gathering and welcome to the assembly

Leader: As we gather at the end of another academic year we come to remember and to recall all that this year has brought in to our lives. At our opening assembly we were invited in our reading to 'shine like stars for all the world to see'. Our stars and candles remind us of that day in September when we accepted God's invitation to shine in the darkness of our world …

Let us take time to reflect on those times and occasions when our star shone for all to see …

For some of us we were the stars of the sports field … a member of the victorious school team bringing home the trophy …

For others a time to shine came on the stage … in the school musical production … or in the musical evening …

For others it was our organisational skills that shone through as a member of the school student council … as a prefect … as sports captain …

For others still it was in school and state exams … gaining high marks …

Perhaps some of us shone in other ways … as a good friend … as one who cared … as young scientists … as home economists … as artists, musicians or poets …

The school year offers many opportunities to us to shine in many ways … and this is good … it is what school is about … but it is not the end of the story of the star that shines …

Every day during the year we were each offered numerous opportunities to shine in the dark corners …

    To offer a smile to the student who is unhappy…

    To say hello and offer the hand of friendship to the student who is lonely…

To offer help to another student who struggles with a subject ...
To assist a member of staff ...
To become involved in the charity and fundraising activities in our school ...
To join a group that offers help to others (schools may name particular groups) in so many ways ...
To be the one who shows initiative in taking care of our school environment ... collecting the litter ... collecting the recyclables ...

These are just some of the ways we may have been the star that shone in the world this school year as an example to others ...

So as we prepare to go our separate ways ... as we look forward to holidays let us remember that we are constantly invited to shine like the stars ... not only in school but everyday whether at home, at school or away on holiday ... the invitation from God remains ...

We take with us this quotation from the Book of Genesis:

Reading: Genesis 1:15
'Let there be lights in the expanse of the sky to give light on earth.'
(repeat 2 or 3 times)

So we pray for each other that we will seek always to be the light in the sky shining for others, lighting their way through the darkness of the world. Amen.

Opening of Year Assembly
Gifts

Setting: centre piece with many different shaped boxes/parcels wrapped in a variety of coloured paper – tied with bows and ribbons

Gathering and welcome (background music – optional)

We all love to receive a gift ... be it for our birthday ... Christmas ... Easter eggs ... First Holy Communion ... Confirmation ... a gift to say thank you ... to say 'I love you' ... to congratulate us on an achievement ...

We all give gifts to others to mark special occasions ... giving and receiving goes on every day in all parts of the world ... in every family ... in every friendship ...

Our parcels here remind us of these gifts ... when a gift is offered we often try to guess what it contains ... we might shake it, feel it ... we are filled with wonder and expectation as we wait to open it ... we love the excitement of ripping off the paper and discovering the contents ... we love the surprise the gift offers ...

Gifts remind us that we are loved ... that someone cares enough to go to the trouble of choosing something especially for us ...

Throughout our lives we will continue to give and to receive gifts from many people for many special reasons ...

But today let us think more deeply about 'gifts' ...

Throughout our lives we receive many other gifts ... the gift of music ... the gift of knowledge ... the gift of courage ... of wisdom ... we recall on our Confirmation day being gifted with the seven gifts of the Holy Spirit ... do we remember what they are called? ... what they call us to be and to do?

As we begin this new year let us reflect on the gift we can be to each other ... as we welcome our new students we give thanks for the gift they are to our school ... the gifts they will bring to our school community ... we remind ourselves of the gifts we know each other possesses ... gifts we have been grateful for in past years that we know will once again be offered to us in this coming year ...

We each are given a variety of gifts by God to use in the service of others ... each one of us is unique ... each of us has gifts that are particular to us ... let us make a commitment today to use our gifts for the benefit of our school community this year ... to make it a place of welcome for all ... a place where every student is valued for who they are and the gifts they bring to our school ... we need to acknowledge the gifts in each person and allow them to use their gifts for the good of all in order for our school community to grow and flourish during this year ...

We remind ourselves of the words of St Paul speaking to the early Christian community when he says:

Reading: 1 Corinthians 12:4-7
There are many different gifts, but it is always the same Spirit; there are many different ways of serving, but it is always the same Lord. There are many different forms of activity, but in everybody it is the same God who is at work in them all. The particular manifestation of the Spirit granted to each one is to be used for the general good.

Prayer
Let us pray in thanksgiving for the gift of each person here ... we give thanks to God for the gifts they bring to our school community and we pray that during this year we will flourish and grow in love and service of each other as we use our gifts for the benefit of all people. Amen.

End of Year Assembly
In Thanksgiving for the Gifts

Setting: Return to the centre piece from the opening of the year – the selection of wrapped parcels in a variety of colours and wrappings. Now open some of the parcels – perhaps leave some with the wrapping paper partially torn off)

Gathering and Welcome (you may choose to use background music)

Let us remember back to the beginning of this academic year when we gathered and took as our theme for the year 'gifts' – the gifts we have, the gifts of others that we receive and celebrate – the gift of each of us to the other – the gifts we use in the service of our school community ...

How and when did you use your gifts during this year?

The gift of music ... in the orchestra ... the choir ... in the school musical production ... in times of celebration of liturgy ... at party time ...
The gift of knowledge ... achieving good results in exams ... helping another student who was struggling with homework or exam preparation ...
The gift of a friendly smile and a cheery few words to the student who was lonely or lacked friends ...
The kind words to another who was going through a difficult time ...
The gift of sportsmanship ... playing on the school teams ... helping to win the match ... encouraging others to play their best ...
The gift of creativity ... using your artistic talents to beautify our surroundings ...
The gift of caring for others ... looking out for fellow students, that they are well and happy in our community ...

These are just some of the gifts we have used in the service of our school community this year and also are the gifts we have received from each other at different times during the year ...

We recall that each of us is unique … a unique gift of God to our world … to the people we come into contact with … to the places where we find ourselves … all this is part of God's plan for us …

Today is a day to give thanks for the gift of each other … for all that we have been to and for each other during the year … to remember those people who have been there for us at just the right moment … to give thanks for all who have helped us … supported us … encouraged us on this year's journey … and to pray for each other as we go our separate ways for the summer holidays …

Especially today we give thanks for those who will leave our school community for the last time … their days here are over … but they will be remembered for all they have generously given to our school community … for all they have been for us during the time we have shared together here in this school … we say thank you to them for their gifts which they have put at the service of our school to help us to grow and flourish as a community … we have all benefited from their generosity during their time here …

And as we remember we say thank you … in the words of Saint Paul as he wrote the Philippians so we too pray:

Reading: Philippians 1:3-6
I thank my God whenever I think of you, and every time I pray for you all, I always pray with joy for your partnership in the gospel from the very first day up to the present. I am quite confident that the One who began a good work in you will go on completing it until the Day of Jesus Christ comes.

Prayer:
Lord, as we pray in thanksgiving today for the gifts we have received and for all that we have shared together, we ask your blessing on each of us as we break for the holidays and especially on those who leave us today. May God who worked through us in our lives this year remain with us in to the future as we seek to continue to live the gospel message in all its richness. Amen.